(North)

KEY

 1 Roman Catholic Cathedral
 2 Holkham House
 3 George Borrow's House
 4 St Benedict's
 5 St Swithin's
 6 St Margaret's
 7 St Laurence's
 8 St Gregory's
 9 St Michael-at-Coslany
10 St Mary-at-Coslany
11 St George Colegate
12 Bacon's House
13 Octagon Chapel
14 Old Meeting House
15 St Clement's
16 Norwich School of Art
17 St Andrew's and Blackfriars' Halls
18 St Peter Hungate
19 Augustine Steward's House
20 St Simon and St Jude
21 Maid's Head Hotel
22 Edith Cavell statue
23 King Edward VI School
24 Cathedral
25 Cotman House
26 St Martin at Palace
27 St Edmund's
28 St Saviour's
29 Norwich Puppet Theatre, St James's
30 Adam and Eve P.H.
31 Great Hospital
32 St Helen's
33 Cow Tower
34 Pull's Ferry
35 James Stuart Garden
36 Duke of Wellington statue
37 Admiral Lord Nelson statue
38 Erpingham Gate
39 Ethelbert Gate
40 St George Tombland
41 St Michael-at-Plea
42 Armada House
43 Suckling House
44 Bridewell Museum
45 St Andrew's
46 St John Baptist Maddermarket
47 Strangers' Hall
48 Maddermarket Theatre
49 Friends' Meeting House
50 St Giles'
51 Churchman House
52 City Hall and Police Station
53 Theatre Royal
54 Assembly House
55 St Stephen's
56 Sir Thomas Browne statue
57 St Peter Mancroft
58 Guildhall
59 Castle
60 Shire Hall
61 St Peter Parmentergate

☐ Pedestrianised areas

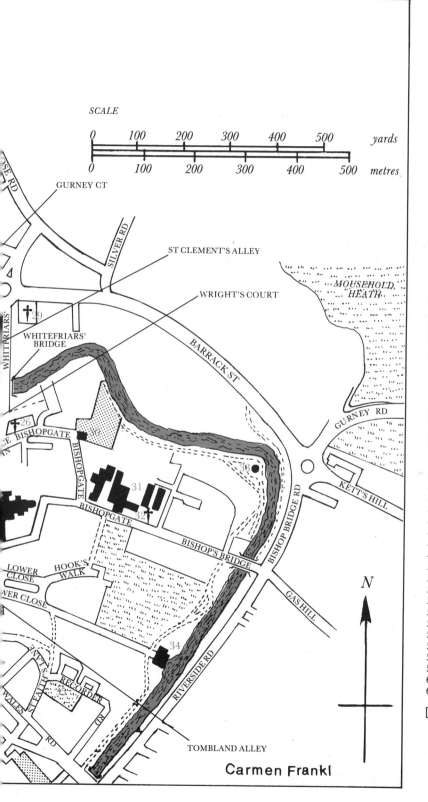

SCALE

GURNEY CT

ST CLEMENT'S ALLEY

WRIGHT'S COURT

MOUSEHOLD HEATH

WHITEFRIARS' BRIDGE

BARRACK ST

GURNEY RD

BISHOPGATE

KETT'S HILL

BISHOPGATE

BISHOP'S BRIDGE

BISHOP BRIDGE RD

LOWER CLOSE

HOOK'S WALK

GAS HILL

N

RIVERSIDE RD

RECORDER RD

TOMBLAND ALLEY

Carmen Frankl

NORWICH

NORWICH

Text by
C.V. ROBERTS

With photographs by
ERNEST FRANKL

THE PEVENSEY PRESS
Cambridge England

Published by The Pevensey Press
6 De Freville Avenue, Cambridge CB4 1HR, UK

Acknowledgements
Permission to take photographs of interiors has kindly been given
by those in charge of many buildings in Norwich, including
permission given on behalf of the Dean and Chapter of Norwich
Cathedral, and the Vicar of St Peter Mancroft. All these are
gratefully acknowledged.

Map: Carmen Frankl

Edited by Julia Harding

Designed by Jim Reader and Sarah Carmichael

Design and production in association with
Book Production Consultants, Cambridge

© Ernest Frankl and The Pevensey Press, 1989
First published 1989

ISBN 0 907115 53 5 hc
     0 907115 54 3 pb

Origination by Anglia Graphics
Typesetting in Baskerville by Textype Typesetters, Cambridge
Printed in Hong Kong by Mandarin Offset Ltd

Front cover The soaring late-15th-century spire of Norwich
Cathedral, second in height in Britain only to that of Salisbury,
seen across the immaculate sward of Almery Green.

Frontispiece (**1**) A penance in stone: soon after 1300 the citizens of
Norwich were ordered by the King to build the Ethelbert Gate,
the upper of the two gates into the Cathedral Close, in reparation
for their attack on the Cathedral and priory in 1272. The
elaborate pattern of flint and stone – known as flushwork – on the
pediment is a 19th-century copy of the original.

Back cover Norwich Castle has dominated the city for nine
hundred years; the crisp facade it presents today is essentially a
Victorian reconstruction, in sharp contrast with the raw Norman
interior.

Contents

Introduction

Look at a modern street map of Norwich, and, even with the great changes of the last couple of centuries, you can still see that all roads lead to Tombland, the curiously shaped space outside the Cathedral gates.

This is no accident, for a thousand years ago Norwich began here – not, as it would seem, around the great central market place bounded by Castle and City Hall. Here was the focal point of the original Norwich, the 'tum-land' or open space (nothing to do with tombs) around which Saxon bands established their rough and ready settlements. As far as is known, they were three in number – Northwic, Westwick and Conesford: the first name developed into 'Norwich', the last two still live on in streets and political wards of the city.

Who these people were is unclear. The idea has been advanced that they were stragglers fresh from the final sacking and destruction of the old Roman town of Venta Icenorum, the modern Caistor St Edmunds a few miles out of the city. But that may be the stuff of fancy.

What is clear is that this open space became the market place, stretching beyond the Maid's Head Hotel at its lower end to the river and modern Fye Bridge, and east towards the site of the Cathedral. In place of the fine 18th-century houses (**4**) opposite the Cathedral gates (**1**) stood the palace of Gyrth Godwinsson, Earl (Eorl) of East Anglia and brother to King Harold II, who in the years before the Norman Conquest of 1066 ruled over some 5500 souls. Records relate that Harold's immediate predecessor, King Edward the Confessor, exacted annually from this fledgling town a tax of £20, six jars of honey, one bear and six dogs for baiting.

With the coming of the Normans, the focus of Norwich was abruptly changed, away from the original centre to what has remained the city's principal square. They established there a new market, and overlooking it built their castle – timber at first, the present stone keep followed in 1120–30 – massively increasing in height the Saxon artificial mound. Thus they created a power point from which to intimidate the native and rebellious populace. So much for the charming and confident assertion of George Borrow that in the heart of the mound sits an old heathen king 'with his sword in his hand and his gold and silver treasures around him'. (It was from Borrow, author of *Lavengro* and *Romany Rye*, that modern Norwich borrowed the sobriquet seen on all the boundary signposts, 'A Fine City'.)

The Normans struck their next blow at the old Saxon centre when they drove the great boundary wall of their new cathedral priory through the very centre of the old tum-land. This was the first move in an increasingly bitter relationship between town and priory which, two centuries on, would peak in a pitched battle, in huge destruction, and in a savage visit by the King himself to restore order.

2 *Norwich Cathedral, begun by the Normans: the nave from the east, showing the medieval choir stalls and part of the splendid 15th-century roof.*

Yet Tombland doggedly remained a principal hub of the growing town, for from here the small original settlements had extended north and south along what are now King Street and Magdalen (pronounced Mag-da-len in Norwich) Street, creating a line which is visible even on today's street map. Neither Norman power nor priory obstruction was able to change that. None the less, the centre of government moved to the area where it still holds sway – first to the Castle, then the Guildhall, and, in modern times, the City Hall.

The story of Norwich is a complex and fascinating one, and in the account which follows – beginning at the Castle, which moulded the shape of the city today, and ending at the Cathedral, which in its own way has never ceased to dominate the place – the object has been to tell this story through the evidence which can still be seen. This is a city rich in buildings from every period of its thousand-year history. In the surge of 'development' and 'modernisation' of the 1950s and 1960s, when Britain's towns and cities lost so much of their heritage, Norwich fared better than most. For then as now, it was fortunate in having a city government which cares about heritage, about the historic face of the townscape, and which has consistently restored and preserved fine buildings – though in the late 1980s central government restrictions on expenditure have slowed the process.

In conservation terms, an overriding problem has been presented by Norwich's medieval churches. Even today there are 32 of them, more than in any other city in western Europe. In 1967 Bishop Launcelot Fleming

3 *For nine hundred unbroken years, since it was established here by the conquering Normans, the market place has been the heart of Norwich city life. Beyond the multi-coloured stalls stands the Guildhall, now the tourist information centre.*

4 *No. 5 Tombland, one of the fine 18th-century houses on the site of the palace of the Saxon Earls of East Anglia and facing the wall of the Cathedral Close, which the Normans built across the original Saxon market place.*

appointed a commission led by Lord Brooke of Cumnor to advise the diocese on the right solution for their use. The commission, in a decision which continues to cause reverberations, concluded that 24 of these churches 'would seem no longer to be required for Church of England parish use'. In the wake of the commission, 17 churches are now officially redundant, and in the care of the Norwich Historic Churches Trust. Two of the 17 are still used for worship, though not as Anglican parish churches. For the majority of the others, alternative uses have been found.

An increase in vandalism and theft has unfortunately required most of the still 'living' churches to be locked, and only a few of the redundant ones are readily accessible. In some cases a notice at the door indicates where a key can be found; persistent visitors will usually track one down. Descriptions of the churches in this book quote dates wherever possible. Where precise records are not available, the architectural periods are given: Norman (1066 – *c.* 1200), Transitional/Early English (1200–1300), Decorated (1300–1350), Perpendicular (1350–1500) and Tudor (1500–1600).

9

A Tour of the City

(A map of Norwich detailing our route around the city is shown on the front and back endpapers)

From the Castle to Charing Cross

Our tour into Norwich's past, and around the city today, begins at the **Castle** (**5**), though what is seen now is a far cry from what the Normans constructed; they created enormous earthworks and ditches, of which a vestige can be seen in the Castle Gardens. Its lifetime as a military castle, however, was relatively short. From 1345 to 1887 it was the county gaol. Public executions were carried out by the bridge over the 'ditch' – the last being in 1849.

The too-perfect orderliness of the façade which the Castle keep presents today dates back to 1834, when the architect Anthony Salvin refaced it in Bath stone in a 'restoration' which exhibited more enthusiasm than sensibility – and, as the files of the local newspapers of the time show, created a storm of controversy. In 1894 it became the **Castle Museum**, opened by the Duke of York (the future George V). The excellent art gallery contains in particular the finest collection of works of the Norwich School of painters, an important English regional school of landscape painting which flourished in the first half of the 19th century. Its masters were the elder John Crome (1769–1821) and John Sell Cotman (1782–1842), with some nine principal followers. They were almost exclusively landscape painters in oils and water-colour, dealing largely with Norfolk scenery.

After Salvin's composed exterior, the inside of the Castle keep, said to be the fifth largest in England, comes as something of a shock – here are the raw Norman walls, powerful and impressive. The present gallery marks the height of the original 'living floor', which accommodated the garrison on one side and, on the other, divided from them by a wall, the Governor and his family. Below the living level, on the present floor of the museum, were the stores and horses, and the tiny chambers set within the thickness of the walls were probably lavatories. The keep now serves as the centre-piece of this outstanding museum of archaeology, geology, and natural and social history.

A patient climb up a corkscrew staircase to the battlements (open in summer) leads to a superb view of the city and the county beyond, leaving no doubt as to how well placed the Normans were to oversee the market place and town.

Look leftward from this vantage: the car-park between the Castle and the modern Eastern Counties Newspapers building, with its time and temperature digital 'clocks', was for three hundred years the city's cattle market, which weekly brought Norwich to a miry standstill – until the dislocation and manure could be tolerated no longer. In 1960 the cattle market was moved out to a new, spacious site on the city outskirts at Harford Bridges. In a great new development plan due to begin in 1989, the car-park will go underground and a green park will take its place, and shopping malls and

5 Norwich Castle presents a Victorian Bath-stone face to the city – the result of a major restoration in 1834. The keep interior, however, is raw Norman. The Castle is now a superb museum and art gallery.

hotels will bound it between E.C.N. and the old Bell Hotel, in the right foreground.

The Bell stands on Orford Hill (known as Hog Hill in former days), and dates back before 1600. But in the 18th century it was famous, or notorious, for two things – its celebrated cockpit and its Hellfire Club. The latter specialised in an idiosyncratic blood sport: its members were a group of ruffians who called themselves 'gentlemen of principles inimical to government, and with a determination to crush the Methodists'. Their operations were particularly directed at John and Charles Wesley, who made their first visit to Norwich in 1754, but other preachers were equally subjected to violence and disruption, either by the 'gentlemen' or by their paid bullies. In 1793 the Bell also became the haunt of a revolutionary society which met there to celebrate the French Revolution.

Up and right from the Bell, from the vantage of the Castle, the eye takes in the Perpendicular splendour of **St Peter Mancroft Church** (**6**). 'Magna crofta' was the great field below the Castle on which the Normans settled the market, before building their own church alongside it on the St Peter's site and establishing what was for several generations the French quarter of the town. Such divisions as Saxon and French were gradually forgotten and all became citizens of one increasingly prospering city, though three centuries were to pass before it was granted the right of self-government.

The original St Peter's gave way to the present church, a superbly composite building completed in 25 years (1430–55) and virtually unaltered since then. The only additions are the late-19th-century parapets and corner pepper-pots on the tower, and the slightly later miniature spire. The tower, lush with panelling, niches and flushwork (a particularly East Anglian speciality of knapped flint set flush into patterns of brick or stone), is a little too much – 'more rich than aesthetically successful', as Nikolaus Pevsner put it. But the body of the church is wonderful: clean, soaring lines and huge windows, including a remarkable clerestory of 17 windows each side (**8**).

The fine, steeply sloping site made possible a passageway under the chancel which, with the open arches under the tower, made a processional way within consecrated ground. In medieval times church processions were an important part of services on Sundays and Feast Days: crosses and banners were paraded around the building, and between the representations of the 14 Stations of the Cross within. St Peter Mancroft and St Gregory's Church in Pottergate are rare in having these exterior 'ways' within their own bounds.

Inside the church, the light pours in, accentuating its great height and space, and lighting the beautiful hammerbeam roof. A Civil War gunpowder explosion nearby destroyed most of the church's medieval glass, and later what was left was collected together and placed in the east window (**7**). It presents a truly outstanding example of the surviving work of the Norwich School of glass-painters, a remarkable burgeoning of this art which began in the late 13th century and reached its summit in the 15th. Indeed, in the late Middle Ages, Norwich was one of the leading centres of English art, producing not only glass-painters but artists working on screens, roofs and walls. The Mancroft window offers a beautiful and fascinating array of New Testament themes, alive with medieval detail. A close inspection, aided by binoculars, is recommended.

On the south wall of the sanctuary is a restrained and elegant memorial to Sir Thomas Browne, the celebrated physician, scientist, writer, scholar, antiquarian, sage and philosopher, who was knighted in 1671 during a royal visit to Norwich by Charles II, in recognition of his steadfast Royalist loyalty. Norwich stood solidly for the Cromwellian cause in the Civil War, and when the citizenry was pressed to provide funds for the raising of a new Parliamentary army, Browne refused to contribute.

His writings are renowned for their rich and sonorous prose, not least in *Urn Burial*, in which he considers the various ways of being interred. Nearby, on Hay Hill, behind Mancroft Church, a statue of Sir Thomas sits on a plinth, contemplating in his right hand a broken urn. Long after he died, in about 1840, his skull was filched by the Norfolk and Norwich Hospital – in a 'scientific enquiry' about the size of his brain – but it was returned and re-buried below his memorial in 1922; a stone marks the spot.

Between Mancroft Church and the provision market is a picturesque old pub and one-time butcher's shop, the Sir Garnet Wolseley, named after the distinguished veteran of the Ashanti and Zulu Wars of Victoria's reign, who raced to relieve General Gordon at Khartoum in 1885 but was too late by two days to save that curious man's life.

The building which dominates the market place is the **City Hall**, whose clean Scandinavian lines, though striking, have never attracted universal approval in Norwich. It was designed by C.H. James and S.R. Pierce, and opened by George VI in 1938. Nikolaus Pevsner fulsomely described it as 'likely to go down in history as the foremost English public building of

6 One of the landmarks of the city, St Peter Mancroft Church (1430–55), dramatically floodlit at night.

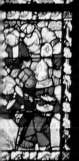

8 *Looking east down the south aisle of St Peter Mancroft Church towards the St Anne Chapel.*

7 *Fine medieval glass in the east window of St Peter Mancroft Church, an outstanding example of the surviving work of the Norwich School of glass-painters.*

between the wars'. The fine bronze doors merit close attention: their bas-reliefs by James Woodford show the city's industries, past and present, and key events in its history.

Facing St Peter Mancroft Church across the market place is the **Guildhall** (**3, 10**), in striking patterns of stone and flint, built on the site of the Norman tollhouse. It is almost contemporary with St Peter Mancroft, for it was begun in 1407, and was constructed by local forced labour. For 530 years thereafter, it was the seat of city government, presided over by 529 successive mayors and lord mayors, until the administration moved over the road to the new City Hall in 1938. Here too sat the assize court; and, until very recently, the magistrates' courts, before they moved to custom-built premises off Bishopgate.

In 1908 this handsome old building came within a hair's breadth of being demolished – but was saved by the Mayor's casting vote. Today, appropriately, it is the city's tourist information centre. The old council chamber (**9**) has a carved Tudor ceiling and 15th-century stained glass in one window. On the floor below is a newly furnished display room for the city's fine regalia, the Spanish Admiral's sword which Lord Nelson presented to the city after the Battle of St Vincent in 1797, and other items of Nelson memorabilia. Below ground are the crypt and dungeons, with traces of manacles still in the walls. Here, in 1549, after the failure of his rebellion, Robert Kett spent his final hours before being taken to the Castle for execution. More summary justice, if local lore can be believed, was meted out outside the Guildhall at the corner

pointing towards City Hall: the iron ring bolt and staple set in the wall there are said to have been used to secure miscreants before they were publicly flogged.

The opulent doorway to the right of the ring bolt is not an original part of the Guildhall, but was taken from a house in nearby London Street, where it was the entrance to the home of John Bassingham, a goldsmith in the reign of Henry VIII. When the house was pulled down in the mid-19th century the doorway was brought here.

Long before the fine 18th-century houses were built behind the Guildhall and along the lower side of the market square, this area immediately below the Castle was the Jewry, where the Jews were nominally under the protection of the Norman governors – as long as they provided necessary capital. Such protection did not save them from violent anti-Semitic riots in 1144 and eventual scattering in the pogroms of Edward I around 1300, in which he indulged at the insistence of Holy Mother Church.

Later this area became predominantly one of coaching inns, facing onto the square and backed by their stables, muck heaps and sewers – the name of the little crooked street off the square, Back of the Inns, perpetuates that fact. Only one of those inns remains, the Lamb, found down the alleyway which links Orford Place and Haymarket, with a pleasant yard in front of it. When the Jews were removed and their property sequestrated, the Church was among the beneficiaries. One of the Jewish buildings was granted to the Mass of Jesus, a foundation in St Peter's Church, and when later transformed into an inn was given the sign of the Holy Lamb.

9 Renaissance linenfold panelling behind the Mayor's seat in the old council chamber of the medieval Guildhall.

10 The Guildhall, begun in 1407. This south-east face, surmounted by a mid-19th-century clock turret, is a particularly good example of East Anglian flintwork.

The Lamb has its own stories to tell. In 1843 Norwich and the surrounding countryside were struck by thunder and a hailstorm of tremendous violence, which brought appalling flooding and damage. Under the mantelpiece of one of the bars in the Lamb is a small brass tablet showing the high water mark of the flood. The entire city centre was under water, and ice from the hailstorm lay 4–5 inches deep. At two o'clock the next morning the storm began again, with equal violence. As the *Norfolk Chronicle* graphically described: 'A surface of flame spread across the heavens, followed by a clap of thunder which seemed to rend the welkin.'

The outcome of all this was the splendidly named General Hailstorm Society, an insurance company founded that same year by a Norwich worthy, Charles Suckling Gilman. Thirteen years later he and his son, Charles Rackham Gilman, began the Norwich and London Accident and Casualty Assurance Association. In due course these enterprises were absorbed by another, and older, local insurance society whose beginnings go back to 1797 – now a vast, worldwide giant known to all as the Norwich Union.

One of the links for walkers and shoppers between the market place and Back of the Inns is the **Royal Arcade**, a notable architectural eccentricity which, though Victorian in date, is thoroughly Edwardian in spirit. Between 1985 and autumn 1988 it underwent a massive restoration which has greatly improved its shops without in any way damaging its character. Jonathan Mardle (pen name of Eric Fowler), who for more than 30 years was the revered essay writer of the *Eastern Daily Press*, described the arcade in 1958, when it changed ownership: 'The architect was George Skipper, who...built Moorish arches, faced with white tiles, and enriched with coloured faience ware. He imported Italian workmen to lay the tesselated pavement, and over the shops, the walls and the glass roof he fairly let himself go in the style called Art Nouveau.'

Jews, coaching inns and great private houses may have gone from the quarter of Norwich between Castle and market place, but the open **market**

(**3**) remains, still the colourful heartbeat of Norwich that it has been for nine hundred years. Today it is fairly relaxed about who sells what and where. Not so in medieval times. Here in orderly 'rowes' of wooden 'selds', or stalls, running north and south, with Middle Rowe down the centre, were glovers, mercers (textile and silk merchants), needlers, lorimers (goldsmiths) and apothecaries; there were the hay, poultry and herb markets; and where the steps of the City Hall are now were sold bread, barley and grain, and even mustard.

Until about 1400, when the city clamoured for its own independent government and was granted its Charter by Henry IV, this kaleidoscopic market and the surrounding township were ruled by bailiffs, as they had been since the Conquest. These gentlemen were elected in the Hall of the College of St Mary, one of the considerable number of religious houses and institutions which punctuated Norwich at that time. On the site of that college today, over beyond the tower front of St Peter Mancroft and set back behind elegant wrought-iron gates and railings (1902) and neat lawns, is the **Assembly House** (**13**) in Theatre Street.

Used with pleasure by many thousands of people each year for its restaurant, concerts, exhibitions and meetings, the Assembly House nevertheless retains the reserved air of a noble 18th-century mansion. It was built in 1754 by the local architect Thomas Ivory between the two wings of a 17th-

13 *Norwich's Assembly House, an 18th-century mansion built between the two wings of a 17th-century house on Theatre Street, is now the home of concerts, exhibitions, meetings and a popular restaurant.*

14 *The elegant entrance hall of the Assembly House.*

century house, which are still there; the wing to the right accommodates one of the most intimate and attractive cinemas in England. The original house was built by the Hobarts of Blickling, who joined the blue-blooded scrabble for monastic land after the Dissolution and placed their new town mansion with its forecourt where the cloisters of the College and Hospital of St Mary had been; and all within a park which extended a couple of hundred yards up the street to the pleasant public park which still bears the name of Chapel Field Gardens.

When Ivory's Assembly House opened, the card-playing, dancing gentry of city and county were presented with 'a large ballroom 66 feet by 23 and the small one 50 by 27 feet', as Stacy's *Norfolk Tour* (1808) and his *History of Norwich* (1818) recorded. 'Between them is the tea room 27 feet square, communicating with each other by doors of such construction as to be easily removed, the eye then commands a suite of 143 feet illuminated by 10 branches holding 150 candles; and the company forming into one row may dance the whole length of the building, and then is presented such a scene of beauty and splendour as has few equals.'

For over a century the Assembly House served the select few; then for 60 years it was a girls' school; during the last war it was used by the military. After the war Mr Henry Sexton, a wealthy local shoe manufacturer, bought the building, restored it at very considerable personal expense, and gave it to the city under the care of a trust. The dancers have gone, but something of their spirit lingers on in these finely proportioned rooms (**14**).

Just below the Assembly House in Theatre Street is **St Stephen's Church**, its splendidly eye-catching tower richly patterned and decorated in contrasting flint and stone in roundels, diamonds and window outlines. This was the last of the great series of Norwich churches to be built, the chancel being completed in 1522, the rest some 30 years later, and the tower remodelled in 1601. The body of the church is all Tudor Perpendicular harmony, complemented comfortably by the handsomely embellished tower.

Inside, the great range of 16 clerestory windows makes the hammerbeam roof glow with light. The windows have some notable glass, 16th-century German, Victorian and modern, with a fine St Christopher among the German panels. In the south aisle is an excellent sample of the work of the exceptional Victorian artist in stained glass, C.E. Kempe, showing St Stephen wearing a sumptuous brocaded cloak.

The church contains several good memorial brasses; especially interesting, and the earliest, is one hidden under a little trap door at the east end of the north aisle. It shows the last prioress of Campsey in Suffolk, Elenor Buttry (d. 1546), and at her feet crouch two delightful old bedesmen (almsmen whose job was to say prayers for the souls of their benefactors), clutching their crutches and saying their rosaries against a background of rough grass and flowers.

On the opposite side of the Assembly House is the **Theatre Royal**, the third to occupy this site. As a performing theatre, it has since the early 1970s achieved national and international prominence as that considerable rarity, a civic theatre which breaks-even financially without the help of vast local subsidy – the result of a hugely varied programme and the showmanship genius of its general manager, Richard Condon.

The first theatre, which had opened on 31 January 1758, was 'allowed by all Connoisseurs and Judges to be the most perfect and compleat Structure of the kind in this Kingdom'. By the early 1820s, however, it was in a decrepit state. The Norwich architect William Wilkins, described as proprietor and patentee, undertook the task of rebuilding, at a cost of £6000. That Royal lasted until fire claimed it in 1934, and the present functional building arose the following year.

West of the theatre is **Chapel Fields**, bounded on the far side by a stretch of the old city walls (there are few remnants of these 14th-century fortifications, the best being on Carrow Hill). What an opportunity there was here for a grouping of fine houses – but there is only one to hint how it could have been. This is Chapel Field House on Chapel Field North, three-storeyed, graceful and classical Regency, and characterised, above the white-painted Doric columns of its front door, by a distinctive wrought-iron balcony. Its rear elevation, seen from Cleveland Road, is quite different but equally full of character, being in red brick with a confident, full height, central curved bay.

Having served as pastureland for the great monastic College and Hospital of St Mary, and then, after the Reformation, as part of the park of the Hobart mansion, Chapel Fields later became the Butts, where the compulsory archery of Elizabeth I's time was practised. When the plague hit Norwich in 1666 it was pressed into very different service – as a burial ground for the scores of victims. In the early 18th century it was turned into a reservoir (the water, no doubt, well calcined by plague bones), as the gently sloping sides of the park testify. By 1783 it had become a strolling pleasaunce for all, and in that year *Chase's Directory* declared it to be 'the most eligible situation for a public walk. Here everything that taste and judgement could suggest has been done. Trees planted; walks raised and gravelled; seats placed at certain distances, and even a piece of water formed in the centre' – a remnant of the reservoir?

Beyond Chapel Fields a modern dual carriageway and a vast roundabout have carved through Upper St Giles' Street and reduced it to a cul-de-sac. They have also erased a cheerfully rumbustious bit of Norwich social history. On the west side of the Grapes Hill dual carriageway, welcoming and modernised but still with lots of character, is the Tuns inn. Just opposite, on the east side of Grapes Hill, stood the Grapes inn. At election times in the mid-19th century, the two pubs were the gathering grounds of rival political partisans, the Grapes crowd favouring the 'blues and whites' (the Tories) while the Tuns put their weight behind the 'orange and purples' (the Liberals).

Such political activities had long ceased when the Roman Catholic **Church of St John the Baptist** (**15**; its elevation to cathedral status did not come until 1976) was built opposite the Tuns in the angle of Earlham Road. Designed by George Gilbert Scott and his brother John, it took 16 years to build, funded by the huge generosity of the 15th Duke of Norfolk, and was completed in 1910 – a powerful example of Gothic Revival. Its windows are filled with dense Victorian glass, which gives the vast interior a permanent air of dim religious gloom. A plaque records that from 1827 to 1881 this was the site of the old city gaol, 'which could detain 120 prisoners' who 'were sentenced to work on a Tread Mill, keeping a constant retrograde motion to grind corn'.

A high footbridge takes the walker beyond the Tuns to the amputated head of Upper St Giles' Street, through a busy and attractive street of shops, restaurants and bistros housed in fine buildings spanning two centuries and more, to **St Giles' Church** (**16**) set in a churchyard with a marvellous surround of venerable wistarias. Behind the church, towards Willow Lane, the ground drops away, accentuating the proportions of the tower, which at 113 feet at its parapet (a charming cupola added in 1737 makes it a little taller) is the highest in the city.

The church is largely Perpendicular, almost certainly dating from about 1420–30. The chancel disappeared in the 16th century, but in 1866 the Victorians built a new one, in the Decorated style and wholly in harmony. A curious foible all round the building is the array of massive and magnificently grotesque gargoyles, which again are faithfully echoed on the Victorian chancel. The fine porch has a fan-vaulted roof, the only one of its kind in Norwich.

The interior is splendidly spacious and lofty, and crowned by a particularly good and unusual 15th-century roof. Its beautiful lines lead the eye effortlessly upwards, taking in its archbraced and hammerbeamed construction, and the large-winged angels on the hammers, which bear the coats of arms of England, France and Castile. In the 19th century, by all accounts, the parishioners sat here under umbrellas to protect themselves from the rain seeping in through the roof.

Here too is a pair of fine eagle lecterns; several very good brasses; and a notable collection of mayoral mace- and sword-rests, inscribed with a roll-call of names of 18th- and 19th-century 'First Gentlemen' of Norwich. A curiosity is the cage, or cresset, which in 1549 was installed on top of the church's lofty tower to contain a warning beacon, as Kett's Rebellion eddied

16 *At 113 feet to its parapet, the early-15th-century tower of St Giles' Church is the highest in the city, and its height is accentuated by the church's elevated site at the top of St Giles' Street.*

round the city. There is also an example, rare in this part of England, of the work of the sculptor Sir Henry Cheere: a meticulously carved memorial (1742) to Alderman Thomas Churchman and his wife Deborah.

Just across the road in Bethel Street is the magnificent town house which the Alderman, a wealthy merchant weaver, built for himself between 1725 and 1740. Its perfect proportions, rich red brick and contrasting window frames, with a round-headed classical window over the great pedimented front door, make **Churchman House** (**17**) impressive. Extensive restoration is scheduled by the city authorities for 1989–90, after which the house will become the Norwich Register Office.

A few yards further on round the curve of Bethel Street is the Coach and Horses public house (**18**; restored in 1988), one of the city's most attractive old inns. Look back down the street, and there is the tower of St Giles'; look east and St Peter Mancroft fills the skyline. And there on the wall of the pub are several cast-iron plates which bear the initials, side by side, of MSP (Mancroft St Peter) and PSG (Parish of St Giles'), with dates from 1813 to 1829, and one carved stone slab, let into the wall, dated 1710. These are the boundary marks between the two parishes, and the scene in past days of beating the parish bounds at Ascensiontide. This was always a ceremony of much merriment and horse-play, well fuelled by ale, when 'the commons' could make mock of their betters with (relative) impunity, and 'bumpings and duckings' were the order of the day.

17 *Churchman House, in Bethel Street, the magnificent early-18th-century mansion of Alderman Sir Thomas Churchman, a wealthy merchant weaver whose carved memorial can be seen nearby in St Giles' Church.*

From Bethel Street a little alleyway, Rigby's Court, leads behind the Y.M.C.A. through to St Giles', once the medical quarter of the city. Appropriately, the well-proportioned early-19th-century terrace takes its name from Dr Edward Rigby, surgeon, Sheriff and Mayor, whose 75 years bridged the 18th and 19th centuries (d. 1821). Continue immediately over St Giles' Street into Willow Lane, and the 18th century takes over.

The willows grew on the 'down side' of St Giles' Church, and were replaced by the fine residences which stand there now, forming an impressive downward curve which calls for a foreground of carriages and crinolines. Halfway down on the opposite side is an unhappy sight, the old Roman Catholic chapel and school of 1829, once a handsome, classical building but now sad and dilapidated. At the bottom of the hill, a carefully designed modern development occupies the site of the house of George ('A Fine City') Borrow (1803–81). Where Willow Lane joins Cow Hill another splendid survivor attracts the eye, the elegantly proportioned **Holkham House**, with a small courtyard garden. Its design is attributed to the Norwich architect Matthew Brettingham (1699–1769), and the house was owned by his brother Robert.

The lofty tower of St Giles' adds a dramatic perspective to the view up Cow Hill from this point. It is worth a brief detour into St Giles' churchyard to look at the backs of the Georgian houses which front Willow Lane. They present a confident domestic vista, and the house at the lowest point of the churchyard brings an idiosyncratic touch with its little gothicky oriel window beside a solid Tudor-style door squared off by a plain surround.

At the bottom of Cow Hill is **Pottergate**. To the left, set back on the south

18 The old Coach and Horses pub in Bethel Street, where participants in the merry ceremonies of the beating of the parish bounds stopped to celebrate. Plaques on the wall, partially overhung in summer by flower baskets, mark the boundary between two parishes.

side of the street, are more quietly retiring Georgian houses; Nos. 100, 102 and 104 make a lovely corner group, the last of the trio being particularly pleasing in its symmetry and poise. If you look up Pottergate from this vantage, taking in the excellent 17th–18th-century grouping on the right-hand corner with Ten Bell Lane, the continuing buildings on the left and the old cobbled roadway, it is easy to visualise the impression created in its heyday by this once-important street.

Despite its many survivals, now being lovingly conserved, Pottergate – the ancient potters' quarter – has been through hard times, not least during the last war when this area was devastated by German bombing. Now, like St Benedict's Street, it is experiencing a new lease of life and activity. Moving back towards the city centre, Pottergate meets Upper Goat Lane on the right, the first of a network of ancient narrow streets (several now reserved exclusively for pedestrians) which give a particular character to this part of old Norwich. In the angle of the two is the **Friends' Meeting House**. Built in 1926 to replace an earlier meeting house, its monumental classicism makes it appear much older.

A little further up Pottergate on the left, St Gregory's Alley and its small green, marked by Victorian iron posts, form a charming foreground to **St Gregory's Church**, which now serves as a community arts centre. A good porch, big Perpendicular aisle windows and a most attractive Decorated clerestory make a handsome combination. What is particularly interesting here is that the tall east end is built over an alley which curves and slopes steeply down from Pottergate. It is believed that at one time this was the bed of a stream; later it provided a processional way – as at St Peter Mancroft – around the church. Inside St Gregory's, this construction has resulted in a dramatic range of deep steps up to the sanctuary area, providing a natural stage for the centre's present-day performing arts activities.

At the west end of the north aisle is a large and well-preserved 15th-century wall painting of St George. In the vaulted roof of the porch, a carved boss shows St Gregory (who gave his name to Gregorian Chants) instructing a music class – a fitting motif for the building's new use.

Continuing down Pottergate beyond a group of modern shops, we come to another Georgian 'rescue': notice at first-floor level a delightful Venetian window. The room it lights, now a restaurant, is over the entrance into a courtyard, and is matched by a twin window on the other side. The courtyard itself, now called Bagley's Court, was one of those myriad Norwich yards and alleys which not so many years ago were merely squalid slums and now are bright and attractive with shops and eating places.

Across the road is **St John Baptist Maddermarket Church**. From here, or from the north side through St John's Alley, which passes under the beautiful tower, the church gives real pleasure to the eye as it sits snugly amid its surrounding jumble of venerable neighbours. At the east end, the unusually exuberant 14th-century window tracery looks down onto the narrow street. A chancel, it has been suggested, once extended over this span, its window reused in the rebuilt 15th-century nave. The interior, with slender 15th-century arcades and tall clerestory, is notable for its 18th- to early-20th-century furnishings (especially the Georgian reredos and communion rails, and an early-20th-century screen), for an outstanding collection of brasses dating from 1412, and for a series of excellent monuments.

19 The Maddermarket Theatre in St John's Alley is a Norwich institution. Housed in a former Roman Catholic chapel (1794), it was opened in 1921 as the home of the Norwich Players.

Nearby in medieval times was sold the red vegetable dye prepared from madder roots and used by the Norwich weavers. The **Maddermarket Theatre** (**19**), like its neighbouring church, perpetuates the name. Tucked away in St John's Alley, the theatre occupies an 18th-century former Roman Catholic chapel, and was opened for its present use in 1921 by Nugent Monck. This remarkable man made the theatre, and himself, famous for the presentation and interpretation of the whole Shakespeare canon, played within a theatre which he designed on Elizabethan principles. Today the theatre's blend of amateur players under professional direction continues to flourish, the considerable programme each year presenting a wide range of plays and entertainments from the classical to the modern.

At the bottom of the churchyard is the old pump which formerly doubly watered the parish: it filled the water-spraying carts as well as providing (questionable) drinking water which the first public analyst of Norwich declared lugubriously to be 'pure essence of churchyard'. At the lower end of St John's Alley is a range of fine medieval and Georgian houses, renovated in 1988. The junction here is Charing Cross – Shearer's Cross, originally, and the focal point of the sheep-shearers and cloth-dressers.

The bulk of the new telephone exchange and the multi-storey car-park opposite occupy a site which rings with history and incident. The names of the street onto which the car-park emerges – Duke Street – and the bridge over the River Wensum just beyond – Duke's Palace Bridge – provide the clue.

A vast ducal residence, now wholly disappeared, once occupied this riverside strand, a monument to the pride of the Howards, Dukes of Norfolk, who already owned a selection of properties in Norwich. The first grand palace to stand here was pre-Elizabethan, and entertained Gloriana when she made her triumphal visit to Norwich in 1578. Then a new one was completed in 1671, where Charles II was wined and dined in extravagant luxury. The diarist John Evelyn, testifying to its opulence, recorded that the ducal family lived in princely state and their guests drank from gold goblets; even the fire irons were made of silver.

However, in the opening decade of the 18th century, after a blazing row with the Mayor of Norwich, the eighth Duke, in aristocratic pique, gave orders for his palace to be demolished. He departed in 1711, leaving the building to the breakers, and what remained later became a squalid work-house. Then the last vestige was used as a pub, the Duke's Palace inn, which finally disappeared when the bulldozers moved in during the spring of 1968.

From Strangers' Hall to the Shire Hall

Just to the west of Charing Cross, heading into St Benedict's Street, is a gem of a place which no visitor should miss. **Strangers' Hall** – often taken to refer to the 'Strangers' from France and the Low Countries who came as refugees to Norwich, though this is highly debatable – was last privately owned by a native of Norwich, Mr Leonard Bolingbroke, who bought it in 1904, restored it and formed there the first English 'folk museum'. In 1922, with outstanding generosity, he gave both his collection and the house to the city.

It is, in essence, a medieval merchant's house, centred upon the Great Hall of about 1450 and arranged around a courtyard. Today it is a combination of folk, costume and furniture museum, though that is not a sufficient description, for its various rooms, all gleamingly maintained, are each dedicated to individual periods – Elizabethan, Jacobean/Stuart, Georgian and Victorian.

The house stands upon a stone undercroft of about 1320, and from that time until the 19th century underwent rebuilding and extensions which have given it enormous character and appeal. Nicholas Sotherton, Sheriff of Norwich in 1530 and Mayor in 1539, one of many leading citizens to live here, is thought to have built the king-post roof in the Great Hall, and added the splendid oriel window. A century later another window was inserted to light both the minstrels' gallery, and the handsome staircase, which was added in 1627 by Francis Cock, grocer and Mayor. Decorating the Great Hall is a magnificent series of Flemish tapestries, woven about 1485. Periodically the hall, with the tapestries as backcloth, becomes a memorable setting for concerts of classical music.

Moving west along St Benedict's Street, one becomes keenly aware of the old description of Norwich as offering 'every corner a church, every other house a pub'. St Gregory's, looking down from the left, has already been noted; on the right are St Laurence's, St Margaret's and St Swithin's, the three survivors of the seven churches which used to stand in this one street.

St Laurence's, the subject of a major appeal in 1988, is redundant, unused and crumbling. Yet its size and style are notable: a great Perpendicular tower; a most unusual spirelet on one corner crowning a stair turret decorated all the way down in flushwork; a fine single-hall nave and chancel of the same period, with an impressive clerestory range; and standing apart from the

20 *One of the triumphs of redevelopment in Norwich has been the transformation of the old Bullard's Brewery site and the decayed industrial area around it, in the ancient Coslany area of the city, into an attractive residential district centred on the river.*

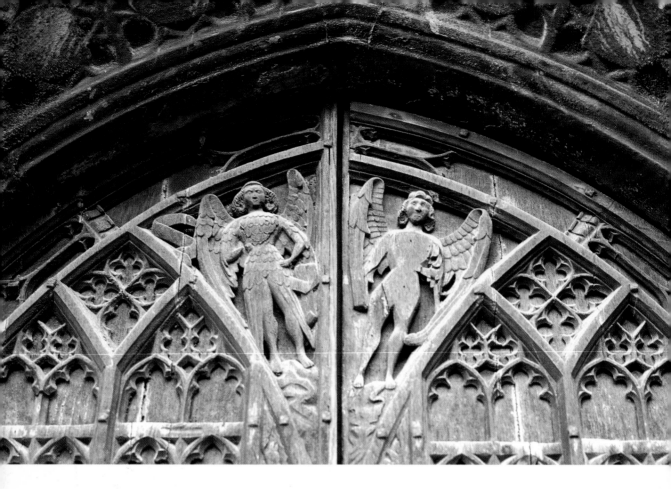

south aisle, a rood stair turret. The church was completed in 1472, most of the money coming from the Abbot of Bury St Edmund's. Descend St Laurence Little Steps (which used to go right down to the river jetty) to view the west door of the tower; just above it on the right the carved subject is the Martyrdom of St Edmund, matched by that of St Laurence on the left. Edmund is here quite pin-cushioned with arrows, while two bowmen drive in yet more. Laurence's death was even more macabre: he shares with St Faith the emblem of a grid iron, for both were martyred by being roasted on one. In this carving you can just decipher the saint laid out, with little figures stoking up the fire below him.

Next along St Benedict's Street is **St Margaret's**, used as a gymnasium club now, a pleasant, medium-sized building with big four-light Tudor windows lighting a brightly spacious interior. The tower is 14th-century Decorated. Facing the street is the two-storeyed porch, where one steps down into the gloom – and gloomy is the story told of the stone seats which run along either wall below the ribbed roof. They are said to date from the era when those who had the job of whipping dogs from the church also had to remove the destitute from the shelter of the porch before the service could begin. As late as 1638, Richard Montague, Bishop of Norwich, was demanding of his clergy in forthright terms: 'Is your communion table enclosed, and ranged about with a rail of joiners and turners work, close enough to keep dogs from going in and profaning that holy place, from pissing against it or worse?'

21 The west doors below the tower of St Michael-at-Coslany are decorated with elaborate traceries and vigorous twin winged figures representing the Archangel Michael and All Angels.

22 The Saxo-Norman tower of St Mary-at-Coslany is the oldest in the city. Luke Hansard, who was to become printer of the journals of the House of Commons (which now bear his name), was baptised in this church in 1752.

After St Margaret's comes the smallest of the three neighbours, **St Swithin's**, now the Norwich Arts Centre (largely professional, whereas St Gregory's is mostly amateur). This neat, plain little building is said to be 15th century although the spirit of the window outlines suggests 14th-century Decorated. The pretty spirelet on the west end was placed there after the tower was demolished as unsafe in 1881.

Almost lost in modern development further ahead to the left, just before the inner ring road, is the solitary round Norman tower, with a no-nonsense 15th-century octagonal top, of St Benedict's – all that was left after German bombers flattened the whole parish one night in 1942.

Down past the west end of St Swithin's Church runs St Swithin's Alley, which must have been quite a squeeze before the tower was removed. There is revealed an attractive thatched cottage, one of the mere handful of thatched buildings now remaining in the city. Sir Peter Seaman, Mayor in 1707, died in 1715 and bequeathed the cottage with other property to fund yearly apprenticeships for two boys from certain parishes. It was saved from demolition and restored just before the last war by the Norwich Amenities Preservation Society, and since 1971 has been in the care of the Norwich Preservation Society.

It is a step now via St Swithin's Road onto Westwick Street, back past St Margaret's towards St Laurence's Church – from here reared up high on its steep embankment – and left into the ancient district of Coslany and **'Norwich-over-the-Water'**. This immediate area is an outstanding example of what can be done to change a depressed, decaying industrial locality into an attractive residential community, full of interesting angles, textures and prospects. Wherever the old could be retained, it has been treated with flair (like the handsome old brewery building in Coslany Street (**20**), immediately opposite St Laurence's, now turned into offices and flats). Where it was necessary to start again, planners and architects have excelled themselves.

Over the river, **St Michael** (also known as St Miles) **-at-Coslany Church** (**21**) is the focal point. It stands amid lawns and trees in a trim square, a superb building belonging almost entirely to about 1500, with soaring Perpendicular lines. Most of all it is a spectacular example of the East Anglian art of flushwork, which an early Victorian commentator likened to 'the inlaid ivory work of old cabinets'. On the south aisle and chapel (the east end of the aisle was built and endowed as a chantry by Robert Thorp, a wealthy merchant in the time of Henry VIII) the flushwork is original; but on the south and east walls of the chancel it is a remarkably clever copy, carried out by a craftsman from Dereham in 1883–4. Today this magnificent building serves as an annexe to the Norwich Amenities Department's Duke Street recreation centre.

Beyond the east end of the church is one of those excellent restorations of a medieval house undertaken by the city authorities, who in Norwich are especially enlightened in this sphere. To the north of the church are **St Miles' Cottages**, a delightful grouping, probably of Tudor construction with 18th- and 19th-century alterations, and now beautifully restored behind their frieze of trees. Past them up St Miles' Steps the road becomes Rosemary Lane (how long since that herb bloomed here?), leading to St Mary-at-Coslany.

But first, on the left, is a wonderful old place, **Pykerell's House**, which used to be the Rosemary Tavern. This 15th-century building and one-time

pilgrims' hall (the principal interior room still has the splendid timbered roof of that time) is in the care of an archaeological trust and is tenanted. It takes its name from Thomas Pykerell, three times Mayor of Norwich in the 16th century.

Pykerell's House is on the edge of the pleasant square – or plain, as such open spaces are known in Norwich – around **St Mary-at-Coslany Church** (**22**, **23**), whose round Saxo-Norman tower, with its distinctive triangular-headed double windows, is the oldest church tower in the city. The nave, entered through a charming two-storeyed porch, was rebuilt in 1477 and is brightly lit by big Perpendicular windows. Today the church serves as a craft and design centre, where well-presented products of high quality are on sale in a welcoming atmosphere.

The spacious churchyard around St Mary's remains railed in, as it has been for decades, for in more leisurely times, when drovers came in from the countryside to markets and fairs and had to 'stop over', their animals were penned here overnight.

East across Duke Street from St Mary's Plain, Muspole Street leads into the heart of an old quarter which, after the decline of the textile trade, and later (in living memory) of the shoe industry, was neglected and crumbling. Here again, as at Coslany, new life has begun to return, with the same carefully selective restoration (**23**) or sympathetic replacement (**24**).

24 *A handsome example of new development which harmonises with the old city: Merchant's Court, St Gregory's Street. Each summer the shopping mall at the centre of the building is the setting for St George's Music Festival.*

Muspole Street emerges onto Colegate between St George Colegate Church and the Woolpack pub – the latter a real find in Norwich on a summer's day, when real ale and good food, under the shade of the great trees of St George's churchyard, become a particular pleasure. Forget the disused shoe factory looming up behind, and concentrate on the pub itself. What appears to be an agreeable, three-storeyed Georgian building is in fact much older, dating from before the Reformation, when it belonged to the Church. At the end of Muspole Street, behind St George's, is a lovely group of restored 17th-century cottages (Nos. 1–9). Their five big dormers give them a strong presence, and all the windows are now once again complete with their sash frames, giving an added symmetry.

25 Bacon's House, restored in 1978, was the 16th-century town residence of Henry Bacon, a prosperous worsted merchant who was successively Sheriff and Lord Mayor of his city. In the distance is the tower of St George's, between Muspole Street and St George's Street.

St George's itself, compact and comfortable, is one of the churches built in the second half of the 15th century during the city's rising prosperity. In a later and different period of wealth, in the 18th century, the interior was furnished largely as we see it today, with a fine classical reredos, an especially good pulpit, and a substantial west gallery holding a little organ of 1802. The north aisle chapel was built by William Norwyche, Mayor in 1461, and there is a big worn bracket brass (the figures stand on a decorative bracket) to him and his wife Alicia – one of the many fine monuments in the church. John Crome the elder, founder of the Norwich School of painting, lived and died in the parish and lies buried in the south aisle chapel.

Next door, on the corner with St George's Street, is **Bacon's House (25)**, a fine timber-framed building which evokes a time when Colegate (originally

not 'coal' but 'charcoal' gate) was the home of prosperous worsted merchants. It was built by just such a merchant, Henry Bacon, in 1548, no doubt to celebrate his year as Sheriff of his city; later, in 1557 and 1566, he was Mayor. Up at first-floor level on the front of the house, in a moulded stone frame, are two narrow Gothic panels, flanking an elaborate Renaissance shield upon which is Henry Bacon's merchant's mark. Notice also the great wooden door, with its small inner door squared off with prettily carved spandrels (the triangles on either side above the arch).

Before continuing along Colegate, a small diversion between Bacon's House and the church is worthwhile. Halfway down St George's Street, north of Colegate, the short span of Cross Lane leads to Calvert Street. There, almost the only survivor of earlier centuries in its immediate neighbourhood is an attractive gabled house which until 1964 was the Rifleman pub. (It then passed to the ownership of the Franciscan Order, and is now a refuge maintained by the Sisters of All Hallows Community at Ditchingham, in South Norfolk.) Built around 1626, this was by all accounts the tavern frequented nightly by John Crome the elder at the end of a day's work round the corner in his Colegate studio. As a boy he had been apprenticed to a sign-painter, and he kept up this side of his trade; a bill for Norwich inn signs he had painted survives from 1803, when he was at the height of his reputation and could afford to keep a pair of horses to enable him to visit his country pupils:

Painting 'Lame Dog' ....£1 1s. 0d.
Writing and gilding board
      for ye Lamb ....18s. 0d.
Writing and gilding name
      on ye Maid's Head..5s. 0d.

26 *The secluded flower-filled central garden of Doughty's Hospital, just off Golden Dog Lane. This quadrangle of almshouses was founded in 1687 by William Doughty, who bequeathed £6000 for its building and endowment. A thorough restoration and extension came in 1869, and others have followed in this century.*

27 *The remarkable Octagon Chapel (1756), off Colegate, constructed of bricks obtained from 'Mushold' (Mousehold Heath) to a design by the Norwich architect Thomas Ivory.*

Returning to Colegate Street via Calvert Street, we enter a largely 18th-century world of fine houses, several of which arose when this quarter gained in importance from around 1750 as the centre of the flourishing trade in woollens and silks. But there was at this time another element, too, which was to have enormous influence on Norwich: the Quakers were establishing their banking dynasties, with the Gurneys opening their 'banking office' in 1775. Colegate was to become the heartland of the city's Quakers and also of other Dissenters.

The Presbyterian minister John Taylor and his congregation determined to build their own chapel. The result was the remarkable **Octagon** (**27**; 1756), designed by Thomas Ivory, architect of the Assembly House. A little further east along Colegate and up a narrow lane its older neighbour, the **Old Meeting House** (**28**), had been mellowing since 1693 – the meeting place of the Independents, who worshipped in St George Tombland until their first pastor, William Bridge, was ejected in 1662. The Independents were among the ancestors of today's Congregationalists, dating from the Civil War period when Parliament was largely Presbyterian and the army largely Independent. Their chapels were all self-governing and independent of each other, hence the name. Both Octagon and Old Meeting House are distinguished buildings. The former has a dramatic interior, its eight walls contained under an ornate dome; the latter accentuates its symmetrical exterior lines with great brick pilasters crowned by curly Corinthian stone capitals, an overture to the interior of warmly dark woodwork and mellow restraint.

On the south side of Colegate, numerous handsome house-fronts catch the eye. No. 18, Harvey's House, is a finely proportioned building with an especially magnificent front door: Ionic columns support a great triangular pediment and a satyr's head keystone locks the classically rounded arch, which, like its jambs, is richly carved.

No. 20, entered from a small courtyard, has a massive doorway in stone – rare for Norwich – which mixes Greek pediment and Roman pillars. This house dates from about 1600, but was extensively remodelled in 1743. The ground-floor ceiling next to the street is almost certainly original, and rather fine, and the hall and stairway, though much restored, are still impressive in their proportions and plasterwork. Norwich Corporation bought the house in 1972 and restored it. Although it is let to a commercial organisation, visitors are usually welcome to look around.

At the east end of Colegate, on the corner of Fye Bridge Street, is **St Clement's Church**. There has been a church here since the Conquest, and the foundation may be the oldest in the city. But the present building, contained within a trim and pleasant churchyard, is largely Perpendicular, with a Decorated east window. Among its memorials the brass at the east end of the nave commemorating Margaret Pettwode is particularly worth seeing, though worn smooth since her death in 1514. Rather than being presented in the usual stiff, eyes-front position, she turns slightly to the left; her fashionable kennel headdress (a hood wired up to form a pointed arch over the forehead, and with borders framing the face to each side) and parts of her gown were recessed to take coloured enamels, though these, of course, have long since gone.

In the churchyard, near the south side of the church, is the rebuilt tomb of the parents of Archbishop Matthew Parker. He was one of Norwich's most famous sons, who became Elizabeth I's Primate of All England, and worked with courage, wisdom and steady consistency to formulate the tenets on which the Anglican Church still stands. His ideal was 'that that most holy and godly form of discipline which was commonly used in the primitive church might be called home today'. This discipline was carried through into his detailed articles of enquiry concerning ecclesiastical affairs in general and the conduct of the clergy – thus earning him a nickname which has entered the language: Nosey Parker.

Running round two sides of the churchyard is St Clement's Alley, upon whose southern side rears a great, flint-faced house with mullioned windows and topped by dormers. The Victorians may have placed their stamp on it in their restorations and changes, but it is still essentially a 16th-century medieval building, though almost certainly on much earlier foundations.

At its Fye Bridge end St Clement's Alley is occupied by the Mischief Tavern. In the front bar is a 16th-century stone chimney-piece which bears on one end the date 1599 and the merchant's mark of Alexander Thurston, grocer, Mayor of Norwich in 1600, and Member of Parliament the following year, who lived here. His wife's coat of arms is on the opposite end. This curious, up-and-down, nooks-and-crannies place has been a pub only since about the turn of the century, and had at least two names before being given its present one (derived from a long-demolished tavern in nearby Peacock Street) in the 1970s. The original inspiration was the sign by Hogarth for the Mischief Tavern in Oxford Street, London: a man with careworn face,

carrying his wife on his back (with a glass of gin in her hand), a monkey and a magpie (signs of mischief) perched on either shoulder, and around his neck a chain fastened with a padlock bearing the warning 'wedlock'.

Turning away from St Clement's Church and the river, a couple of hundred yards up Magdalen Street we come to **St Saviour's Church**, the only survivor of the six churches which existed on this street when Parker was Archbishop. Now a badminton hall, it still looks curiously rustic and village-church-like, despite its busy urban environment, and must have seemed even more so in the 19th century, when it was thatched. It has a chunky tower with attractive Decorated tracery in its windows, a simple Perpendicular nave without aisles or clerestory, and an earlier, mid-14th-century Decorated chancel with a good reticulated east window (the Latin *reticulum* means a bag of network – the tracery forms a net-like pattern).

An observant dawdle between these two churches reveals what a splendid thoroughfare Magdalen Street used to be, though traffic, signposts and some sorry shop-fronts are a considerable obstacle. Immediately opposite St Saviour's, No. 44, structurally one with Nos. 46 and 47, is complete and fine in its Georgian lines; one of the shop-fronts in the group has delightful 18th-century Venetian windows.

A few yards up to the left from St Saviour's is a narrow passageway which leads to one of those marvellous Norwich surprises. **Gurney Court** is a grandly imposing courtyard of fine houses; here in the 18th century the celebrated Quaker banker John Gurney first set up business. The houses are mainly 17th century and later, in brick, plaster and pantiles, and with dormers facing the passageway. This was the birthplace of John Gurney's daughter Elizabeth, who was to become the zealous prison reformer Elizabeth Fry. Twenty-two years later, in 1802, it was also the birthplace of Harriet Martineau, the economist, progressive journalist, novelist and travel writer, who played an important part in the 19th-century Rationalist movement (which separated science and religion and proclaimed, in essence, that reason was the only way to belief).

Our route now takes us down beside St Saviour's Church, along the unlovely lane of the same name, and turns right into the equally functional Black Friars' Street – its name echoing the presence in Norwich, until the Dissolution of the monasteries 450 years ago, of the Dominican Order of the Black Friars, so called because of their black mantles worn over white habits.

We emerge into Fishergate, formerly the landing place for fish from Yarmouth. Once a populous, noisome and squalid slum, it is now a quiet commercial street. Just one domestic building remains from its 17th-century past, the grey-painted, double-gabled, three-storey house off to the right, which used to be the Duke of Marlborough pub. It was finally saved (after several demolition threats) in 1969, and three years later was restored and converted to a private house. The other reminder of antiquity remaining here is the modest little **Church of St Edmund**, long redundant and sad. It is all of a simple Perpendicular pattern of the 15th century, its particular interest being, inside, 'the curious rhythm' (Nikolaus Pevsner's apt phrase) of the aisle arcade, which is an odd arrangement of openings of irregular heights and widths.

Fishergate meets Whitefriars' beside the river bridge of the same name. In the angle of river and road, now occupied by part of the Jarrolds' printing factory, was the monastery of the Carmelites, popularly known in England as the White Friars because of the colour of their habits. A very small remnant of their great religious house, founded in the mid-13th century, remains within the factory forecourt.

Rearing up behind, and now also part of the Jarrolds' enterprise, is the dramatic height of the old yarn factory (**29**), erected a century and a half ago. This industrial building is magnificent, but is none the less a reminder of a failed endeavour. At that time businessmen here and in Fishergate were trying desperately to restore the declining prosperity of the Norwich woollen trade, which had reached its peak some years before. But by then the drift of the industry to the more thrusting and better-equipped north of England could not be checked: the effort came too late.

From this vantage point, outward from the city and beside the enormous inner-ring-road roundabout, can just be seen the tower of the former St James's Church. This compact building now houses the thriving **Norwich Puppet Theatre**, an interior conversion so complete as almost to hide the original use. But outside it is untouched, entirely Perpendicular with an attractive two-storey porch and a quaint tower, which seems to sit on the building like a turret, but is in fact a true tower, characterised by its brick octagonal top and perky battlements mounted on a square base.

Whitefriars' Bridge, at this river crossing, was opened in 1924 but is the

29 *This unusual and arresting building in Whitefriars' overlooking the River Wensum has been part of Jarrolds' printing works since 1902, but it was originally built by John Brown as a yarn factory in 1836–9, during the desperate but unsuccessful attempt to restore the declining prosperity of the Norwich woollen trade.*

successor of at least five other structures from the 13th century onward. On the 'city' side of the bridge, take the Riverside Walk along the Wensum, heading for the next crossing point, Fye Bridge (**30**), along Quay Side; here in medieval times, local lore has it, was a ducking stool for dampening the spleen of nagging women.

Fye Bridge is said to span the oldest river crossing point in the city. Here a ford may first have been established in Roman times which subsequently served the early Saxon settlements, centred on nearby Tombland. The present bridge was built in the 1930s and is, like Whitefriars', the latest in a long succession going back to the first primitive causeway which negotiated both the river and the marshes to each side.

A few yards up Wensum Street, on the corner with Elm Hill, is **St Simon and St Jude Church**, since the 1950s a centre for the Norwich Boy Scouts Association. A very simple building, without aisles, it has a Perpendicular nave and a 14th-century chancel but is of very ancient foundation – according to tradition it belonged to the bishops before the see was moved from Thetford to Norwich in the 1090s. The church contains magnificent 16th- and 17th-century monuments to the rich and powerful Pettus family. Boxed in to prevent damage, they can be viewed by request during the Scout Shop's opening hours.

Turn now to **Elm Hill** (**31–34**), the city's tourist showpiece. Cobbles, characterful old buildings from the medieval to the Georgian, tactful restorations, and the natural rise of the land to add perspective, give this narrow street the air of a film set. Yet it is as real as flint and seasoned oak. Half a century ago, it and St Simon and St Jude were threatened with wholesale demolition – and were saved very largely through the efforts of the Norwich Society (formed especially for the purpose). Since then this organisation has done much to protect historic Norwich.

In the 15th and 16th centuries Elm Hill (now almost entirely owned and cherished by Norwich Corporation) was very grand, and a busy thoroughfare between Quay Side and the market place. Between the early 16th and late 18th centuries, no fewer than 16 mayors and sheriffs of Norwich had their fine houses there. Almost opposite St Simon and St Jude is one such house, Nos. 34–6, once a single large residence (its central entrance still gives access to a courtyard). To all appearances a handsome Georgian house, it was originally built in 1540, with a lower storey of brick and flint, and an upper storey of plaster and timber.

Just up from the church is Wright's Court, another of the innumerable Norwich courtyards and alleys which have been rescued, beautified and revitalised. Within the courtyard, on the first floor facing the street, is a long weaver's window, designed to give maximum light to a workroom within this ancient three-storeyed building. Appropriately, the court takes its name from Wright & Son, who in the last century had a factory in Elm Hill making 'plain and fancy fabrics' and employing at its peak some fifteen hundred hand-loom weavers.

A little further up the street on the same side, half-timbered and mellow, is **Pettus House** (Nos. 41–3), all that is left of the great late-16th-century mansion of the Pettus family. For years it was neglected and decaying; now it is restored, thanks to the city council – and to help from across the Atlantic from Americans proud to bear the Pettus name. At its grandest the mansion stretched right down to the church which contains the family monuments, and Wright's Court was its carriage entrance to the courtyard.

A short way up the street on the opposite side (Nos. 22–6), superbly restored, stands the great town house which Augustine Steward, a wealthy merchant (whose name recurs frequently in the history of Norwich), built for himself when the great fire of 1507 destroyed the previous mansion. This was Pastons Place, home in the 15th century of the celebrated family of that name, and it was here that a number of the famous Paston Letters were written. For several centuries the enduring Paston clan, who took their name from the village of Paston on the coast, dominated Norfolk. The Letters are a remarkable correspondence by and to members of the family between 1430 and 1503. Their tremendous vitality, their detail, and the picture they give of a tough and dangerous age, still make them fascinating reading.

Today all that remains of their Elm Hill mansion is the courtyard entrance called Crown Court Yard. Over this, on the beam spanning the entrance, Augustine Steward has his merchant's mark, entwined by his initial 'S', carved on the right-hand end; on the other end is a lady in a large flat headdress and a profusion of pigtails. Since 1927, Nos. 22–6 have been home to the Strangers' Club, a gentlemen's luncheon club whose name has no connection with the historical 'Strangers' from the Low Countries who brought their weaving skills to Norwich – but indicates it function, built into its rules, of welcoming newcomers to the city.

Towards the top of the street on the right is another handsome old

31, 32 *Two views of Elm Hill, in earlier times a grand thoroughfare of the city and now an attractive cobbled street lined by buildings of all periods from the medieval to the Georgian.*

grouping, Nos. 12–16. The solid Tudor door in the centre has its own eccentric story. In the 1860s the Rev. Joseph Lyne, who called himself Father Ignatius, intent upon re-establishing the Benedictine Order – but within the Anglican church – began here 'The Priory of St Mary and St Dunstan'. Such were the local passions it aroused that brawlings and bawlings outside this door were a regular occurrence. On one occasion, it is recorded, a thousand people packed the street, determined to destroy the monastery. A 'providential' thunderstorm and lightning scattered them. But if this was divine protection, it was soon withdrawn. Within three years Father Ignatius's priory had passed into history, and the solid red-brick chapel he built behind his house (now part of the Norwich School of Art) became a shoe factory.

Until the coming of Dutch elm disease, a magnificent mature elm stood in the little square outside the good Father's door. All efforts to save it were in vain; now a plane tree (**34**) occupies its spot, and is thriving splendidly. It throws its shade onto the **Britons Arms**, the oldest building in Elm Hill, and the only one to survive the fire which virtually destroyed some seven hundred Norwich houses, including all the ones in this street, in 1507. This thatched 15th-century house, now a coffee shop, was for centuries an inn, and has been in its time the home of nuns, worsted weavers, leather-workers and shoe-makers. For long it was the King's Head. But about 1804, with strong Republican feeling abroad, and the country scandalised by the lifestyles of George III's sons, radical Norwich reacted by changing to a pointedly native nationalist name.

Above the Britons Arms, on the corner with Princes Street, is **St Peter Hungate Church**, established in 1936 as a museum of church art, beautifully maintained and packed with interest. It is all of a simple Perpendicular design, and perfect for its present role, the big windows filling it with light which reflects off the white-painted walls. Replacing an early-13th-century building on the site, the church was completed in 1460 (the date is carved on a buttress of the porch) by John Paston and his wife Margaret, who trod the same square Norfolk tiles which cover the floor today.

On the opposite corner of Elm Hill, the substantial, gabled three-storey 17th-century house (its ground floor occupied by a mouth-watering *pâtisserie*) was extensively restored in 1988, and forms a grand focal point for the descent to St Andrew's Plain. The huge church, now **St Andrew's Hall**, which dominates the plain was the centre-piece of the Black or Dominican Friary, completed in 1471, and was bought by Norwich Corporation from Henry VIII's commissioners at the Dissolution. It is recorded that in 1539, Augustine Steward was instrumental in obtaining the church at a cost of £80 to the city, to serve 'as a fayre and large halle'. This it has been virtually ever since, the great preaching nave of the friars giving way in the last 160 years to an equally inspirational role as the city's principal concert hall and home of one of England's oldest musical festivals, the Norfolk and Norwich Triennial, which began here in 1824.

A vast organ divides St Andrew's Hall from the former chancel of the great church, now **Blackfriars' Hall**. Here, surrounded by an impressive gallery

33 The back of Elm Hill, seen from the Riverside Gardens. Riverside Walk, laid down along the banks of the Wensum in the 1980s, provides an attractive route from which to view the heart of the old city.

of portraits of civic and county dignitaries through the centuries, banquets, meetings, conferences and arts events take place. The restored crypt (now a coffee bar) and remnants of the cloisters are open to view. During the 17th century, Blackfriars' Hall was the church of the Dutch community in Norwich, whose ancestors first began to arrive in the city in the mid-14th century. But it was in Elizabeth's reign that they flooded in, fleeing the campaign of inquisition, death and rapine being conducted in the Netherlands by Spain's barbaric general, the Duke of Alba. Their total number was reported to amount to five thousand men, women and children.

The hardships and horrors shared by both the Dutch from the north, and the French or Walloons from the south, did not, however, bring the two peoples together in the safety of Norwich. Instead they squabbled over who owned the patents for which cloths. But the skills they brought greatly profited the city which took them in, not only in the cloth trade, but in printing (the first printing press in Norwich was set up by a Dutchman) and in silversmithing.

Just around the corner in St George's Street is **Norwich School of Art**, which Geoffrey Goreham described as 'the finest piece of brickwork in Norwich'. Built by the city in 1899 as the Technical Institute, it became the home of the Art School in 1901. Since then its red bricks have warmed and mellowed, though its towering eight-bay spread is possibly a matter of taste.

34 This flourishing plane tree replaced the magnificent mature elm which stood at the top of Elm Hill until it was destroyed by Dutch elm disease. Between the tree and the unspoiled terrace of small three-storey houses a replica marks the site of the original parish pump.

Here, when the place was new, the students included Sir Alfred Munnings, that matchless artist of horses and horsemen and the East Anglian country scene. In one of the studios he discovered the cast of a horse's head taken from the Parthenon. Later he was to write: 'All through the hours at work at lithography from nine to seven I lived only to go on with that splendid horse's head in sepia from seven to nine! The hours spent on it each evening slipped away too fast, but they were not wasted, for I learned all I know of a horse's head from that cast.' The inspirational cast is still in the School's care. In April 1989 the School combined with Yarmouth College of Art to become the Norfolk Institute of Art and Design.

On St Andrew's Plain at the corner with St Andrew's Street stands Garsett House – known in Norwich as **Armada House** (**35**) – a timber-framed building of 1589. Many of the timbers, says local lore, were salvaged from Spanish Armada wrecks on the East Anglian shore. If the house looks lopsided the cause is easily explained: the Victorians, with that blithe disregard for heritage which today is almost impossible to comprehend, demolished more than half of it to make room for their new tramways.

The only virtue of this operation was to open up the view to **St Michael-at-Plea Church** (**35**), with its pinnacled, flushwork tower of the Perpendicular period, and attractive two-storey porch (lively St Michael and dragon carvings appear in the spandrels over the outer door). The spacious nave is lit by large Perpendicular windows, which makes it ideal for its present use as an exhibition hall. The plea 'Forget me not' is inscribed on the clock faces of the tower, but the 'at Plea' in the church's name refers to its former role as the Archdeacon's ecclesiastical court.

Immediately across the road from Garsett House is **Suckling House** with Stuart Hall, housing Cinema City, the city's specialist art cinema. Dating from the mid-14th century, the house takes its name from its former owner Sir Robert Suckling, a rich mercer, who was Mayor in 1572. The honour of the mayoralty was wittily topped six years later when Elizabeth I was in Norwich: she bestowed upon the Sucklings a sprig of honeysuckle as a punning augmentation to their coat of arms. They and their honeysuckle – firmly held in the mouth of a deer – are still around in Norfolk. Suckling House was restored and presented to the city in 1924 by Ethel and Helen Colman, of the famous Norfolk mustard-making family. Here, in March 1927, the Round Table organisation of young business and professional men held its inaugural meeting, presided over by the founder, Louis Marchesi, whose name is perpetuated in a pub a few hundred yards away in Tombland.

Next door, facing St Andrew's Hall, is **St Andrew's Church**, a soaringly spacious church (second only in size to St Peter Mancroft), and still 'live'. The tower was completed in 1478, just seven years after the friars had finished building across the road. The rest was done by 1506 in the full flowering of the Perpendicular style: medieval craftsmanship at its finest. The result is a noble building lit by huge aisle and east windows and by a great range of 11 closely spaced clerestory windows stretching the entire extent of the superb 'single hall' span.

But before going inside, pause in the narrow lane (St Andrew's Hill), below the east window. Here, reset from an earlier church, is a set of shields and coats of arms which is of exceptional interest. First on the left is the double-headed eagle of the Holy Roman Empire, a tribute, presumably, to Anne of

Bohemia, daughter of Emperor Charles IV, sister of King Wenceslas of Bohemia and first wife of Richard II. She visited Norwich with her husband in 1383 and aroused the curiosity of the city by riding to the Great Hospital upon a side saddle, which strange contrivance she introduced into England.

Next come three elongated lions with lashing tails – the arms of England; then the three crowns of St Edmund, used for East Anglia and, temporarily during the Middle Ages, as the arms of Ireland; then the arms of the City of Norwich – three-towered castle and lion; and to their right the Royal arms of England from 1340 to 1405, England's lions being quartered with France's lilies.

The simple 'X' upon its shield is the saltire of St Andrew, beside which is a shield bearing the Instruments of the Passion – a staked cross, scourging post, crown of thorns, spear, reed and sponge, hammer, nails and pincers. Savagely defaced are the three chalices and wafers on the adjoining Shield of the Blessed Sacrament; then comes a simple cross for St George or the Cathedral priory.

Next come individual arms: first Henry Despencer, soldier-bishop of Norwich, who put down the Peasant Rising in Norfolk in 1381. The griffons and chequers are those of Richard FitzAlan, Earl of Arundel; he was joint Governor to Richard II in 1381, but later took a leading part against him and was executed in 1389. Facing towards the Earl's arms is what is believed to be the heraldic beast of Thomas Mowbray, later Duke of Norfolk, who was banished with Henry Bolingbroke (later Henry IV) and died at Venice in 1399. Finally comes a 'ragged cross', whose provenance is unknown.

Inside, St Andrew's Church is all clear, uncluttered lines, with Victorian furnishings, including exuberant reredos, low screen, pulpit and font – and pews with that 19th-century trademark, drip trays for umbrellas! The church is graced by a remarkable number of fine monuments and wall tablets, the Suckling chapel on the north having some of the best of them. The powerfully Protestant temper of Norwich in the early 17th century is illlustrated by two framed canvases at the west end of the south aisle, whose verses leave no room for doubts that the church was 'lately translated from extreme Idolatry …Our noble Queen and Counsell sage Set up the Gospel and banished Popery'.

Local tradition has it that Abraham Lincoln's Norfolk ancestors worshipped here (their principal centre in the county was Hingham, about 20 miles south-west of Norwich, where a bust of Lincoln graces the parish church), so St Andrew's is always an essential on the itinerary of American visitors.

Immediately behind St Andrew's is the **Bridewell Museum**, which since 1925 has displayed the history of four centuries of local industries and crafts – old farm techniques and implements, textile work, the boot and shoe industry, metal working and smithcraft, building, carving, clock-making, and the first wire-netting machine in the world, made in Norwich in 1844. The building itself is of special interest, for its outer wall, opposite the church, is the finest example of squared flintwork facing in the city. Flints are 'knapped' across the middle, with craftsmanly skill, to achieve a shell-like fracture and a lustrous, flat surface. Ideally they should meet on a faced wall with barely a hair-line between them, and in this case they do so superbly, still wonderfully sharp and secure after five centuries.

William Appleyard, first Mayor of Norwich under the new Charter granted by Henry IV, lived here in the opening years of the 15th century, the house having been built 30 years earlier by his father Bartholomew. In 1583 the house became an auxiliary prison – a bridewell – for petty offenders, tramps and beggars, when the Appleyards' spacious merchants' cellars were pressed into dungeon service. (The word 'bridewell' derives from St Bride's Well, a prison in 16th-century London.) After about 1828, the building was used as a tobacco factory before being given to the city in 1923.

Bridewell Alley is one of the most picturesque walkways in the city, one of its attractions being the Mustard Shop, a faithful replica of a Victorian emporium. It was opened in 1973 to commemorate 150 years of mustard milling by Colmans.

Along the top of Bridewell Alley (look back for a magnificently framed view of St Andrew's Church tower) runs Bedford Street, with an agreeable mix of old buildings and attractive shop-fronts. At the top of the incline to the left is London Street, first of the new post-war pedestrian precincts when it was paved in 1965. Without traffic, its handsome, fresh-painted buildings can be fully appreciated.

Occupying a commanding position at the angle of London Street with

36 *On the steeply angled corner of London Street and Bedford Street is what appears to be a classic Wren church, but it was built as a bank in 1928 by F.C.R. Palmer and W.F.C. Holden. It is now the regional flagship of the National Westminster Bank.*

Bedford Street is, on first glance, a splendidly elegant Wren church (**36**), complete with bell turret. Closer inspection reveals it to be a bank – for which purpose it was built, with triumphant confidence of design, in 1924.

Almost opposite is Opie Street (known as 'Devil's Alley' in the 18th century, when sedan chairs used to ply from here). It takes its name from Amelia Opie (1769–1853), whose little cloaked statuette stands on top of a shop on the right, and whose house stood where this small street joins Castle Meadow. Amelia, a noted beauty and popular novelist, married John Opie, the Court portrait painter, and became a very strict Quaker. She and her husband were among the distinguished local figures who at the turn of the 1800s worshipped at the Octagon Chapel in Colegate.

Opie Street emerges into Castle Meadow, the old Castle 'ditches', with the keep rearing up overhead. To the left, the big junction with a plethora of traffic lights is Agricultural Hall Plain, an echo of the days when the countryside dominated the town. The big, red-brick building (1882) diagonally across the plain was the Agricultural Hall, and is now part of the Anglia Television complex, as is the handsome porticoed building immediately below it, to which it has been linked, at the head of Prince of Wales Road. This was at one time the General Post Office, but it began as Harvey and Hudson's Crown Bank (1865), hence the confident sculptured stone crown on its pediment.

The twin roadways of Prince of Wales Road are as Victorian as the two buildings just described. In the autumn of 1843 the railway came to Norwich, with its terminus at what locals still call 'Thorpe Station' (in the parish of Thorpe). To connect it with the city centre, the Victorians merely flattened everything which stood in their way and drove their new road through to join Castle Meadow, thus severing the ancient King Street, which from the very beginnings of Norwich had snaked uninterrupted from Tombland to where the old city walls meet the Wensum (see endpaper map).

At the top of the plain below the Castle Mound, at the junction of Castle Meadow and Market Avenue, stands another Victorian memento, the South African War Memorial, surmounted by a lyrical 'flying angel' with powerfully upraised wings and sheathing the sword of war. Upon the high plinth are the names of three hundred officers and men killed in the conflict.

Behind the memorial is the final piece in this 19th-century ensemble, a large oblong pretending to be a fortified mansion. This is the **Shire Hall** (1822–3), designed in Gothick style by William Wilkins, who was also architect for the National Gallery in Trafalgar Square, London. Originally the centre of administration for the county of Norfolk, it was then for a long period the city's senior court-house. Its future function has been the subject of much lively public debate – perhaps a museum of special interests, headed by military, costume, Nelson and legal collections.

From Market Avenue to the Cathedral

Our route now takes us in front of the Shire Hall, heading up Market Avenue. The sward between here and the new Anglia Television building, and the large car-parks to each side ahead, were until 1960 the cattle market – and also effectively mark the extent in early medieval times of the Castle's bailey or yard.

Follow the road up the gentle incline to join Golden Ball Street in front of the modern Eastern Counties Newspapers building (1969). On the right is **St John the Baptist Timberhill Church**, on whose site a church has stood – just outside the Castle's bounds – since soon after the Conquest. The church was meticulously restored in 1980 and is cared for devotedly, attracting substantial and committed congregations to its High-Church services. Known in ancient times as St John at the Castle Gates, and later as St John by the Timber Market, it was first comprehensively restored in the 19th century, when it was very dilapidated, the tower having fallen down in 1784. The Victorians gave it the trim little bell turret, distinctive tiny dormer windows, and full complement of big Perpendicular-style windows.

In the lovely, spacious interior hangs a fine German chandelier of about 1500; and in the sanctuary is a memorial to the gifted Norwich sculptor Robert Page (thoughtfully crafted in advance by the man himself), who died in 1778, and whose work graces many Norfolk churches. This elegant wall tablet, complete with mourning cherub, is generally reckoned to be one of the best in Norwich. The Stations of the Cross and the Oberammergau rood

37 The massive crown-post roof of Dragon Hall in King Street, a first-floor great hall built around 1450 by Robert Toppes, a rich textile merchant, to display his goods. The two large windows in the north gable wall were inserted by Toppes to illuminate this feat of building craftsmanship. Restoration began in 1987 and a major appeal is now underway to equip the building as a heritage centre for the city and county.

group were restored and recoloured by artists within the church's own congregation.

Just around the corner at the top of Westlegate (anciently Wassail Gate, where, according to tradition, the 'makers of fine white bread for ceremonial occasions' lived and worked) is **All Saints' Church**, a simple building of 14th/15th-century date, combining Decorated and Perpendicular styles. It is now used as a day centre, run by the Mothers' Union as an aid to mothers out shopping and to visitors to the city. Inside are several memorials to the Clabburn family, brewers of porter and great local benefactors in the 19th century. A slate slab on the left of the chancel steps commemorates Thomas Clabburn, who left a legacy to provide bread and coals for the poor of the parish. Today, in an age with new needs, All Saints' continues very much in Thomas's tradition.

Viewed from the junction mid-way between All Saints' and St John the Baptist Timberhill, the broad span of Ber Street, which stretches away to the tower of St John de Sepulchre Church, seems to come to a full halt in front of Timberhill Church. The likely reason goes back even further than the history of Norwich itself. Ber Street occupies a chalk ridge, which provided both a good site and sound foundations for Roman builders to lay down a rammed earth road from their township-camp of Venta Icenorum (today's Caistor St Edmunds). This road led through the site of the future Norwich Castle, down to Tombland and on to a ford marked by today's Fye Bridge. When the Normans came, they did their best to destroy the old Saxon centre at Tombland. They built their castle, the surrounding bailey, and the Church of St John at the Castle Gates, effectively blocking off this communicating way from the south-east, and making their new town centre secure.

Little of that is provable. What is certain is that, centuries on, Ber Street achieved its own kind of importance – and notoriety. This was 'Blood and Guts Street', centre of the butchery trade and, during the three-century reign of the cattle market around the Castle, the 'overflow' and 'parking lot' for incoming farmers, carts, horses and other beasts, all mixed in with the teeming population of Ber Street's squalid courts and alleys. In the 19th century it was such a violent place that the police simply sealed off its ends and left it to its own devices.

At the far end, opposite St John de Sepulchre Church, is Ber Street's one grand survivor, the 18th-century **Ber House**, with three storeys in balanced, confident, Georgian style; 19 large sash windows are complemented by fine portico doorways at either end. In 1988–9 it was thoroughly restored and adapted for use as retirement flats. To each side, settled comfortably against their big neighbour, are restored cottages in Tudor style.

St John de Sepulchre Church (**38**), which dates from 1472, has arguably the most beautiful tower in Norwich. At night, floodlit, it is a glowing gem, with tall clean lines, flushworked stair turret and buttresses 'stepping in' at each level, superb Tudor windows at the height of the belfry and richly ornamented battlements. An elaborate but worn two-storey porch, replete with carved figure niches, shields and flushwork, leads into what is, in architectural terms, a surprisingly simple interior – no aisles, short transepts – relieved by the pure lines of its spacious Perpendicular windows. Within these walls, however, another surprise awaits. St John is now the Norwich church of the Russian and Greek Orthodox congregations, and the Orthodox

38 *A striking view of the beautiful Perpendicular tower of St John de Sepulchre Church (1472), at the south-eastern end of Ber Street. The church is now home to the city's Russian and Greek Orthodox congregations.*

39 *Though its façade is clearly Jacobean, the Music House in King Street is the oldest domestic building in Norwich. It dates from the 12th century, when it was the dwelling house and banking vault of wealthy Jews.*

altar and icons provide a wonderfully exotic complement of variety, colour and atmosphere.

Just beyond Ber House and the church stood the Ber Street gates of the city, which are pictured, with formidable portcullis and towers, on the sculptured sign of the adjoining pub. The city walls, all built in the mid-14th century, ran in a loop whose line is followed now by the inner ring road. There were 12 gateways with fortified towers between them. It is a sad fact that, between about 1790 and 1810, these were demolished wholesale by the civic authorities. On 27 October 1792, *The Norfolk Chronicle* recorded: 'On Monday last the ruthless hands of men began to execute the sentence of demolition passed upon the venerable gates of this city.' The gates were considered an obstacle to traffic movement, and unhygienic. But their original grandeur can be seen in a set of prints etched in 1792 by John Ninham. They were published in a new edition in Norwich in 1861; and a further set (engraved by Ninham's son, Henry) was issued by Jarrolds, the Norwich store and publishing house, in 1864. A selection was reproduced in a booklet in 1982 by the University of East Anglia. (Originals and reproductions can

40 *The Black Tower, on Carrow Hill, named after the black flints from which it is built, is the best surviving remnant of Norwich's mid-14th-century city walls. In 1665–6 it was used as a compulsory isolation house for victims of the plague.*

41 *One of Norwich's outstanding medieval fonts, in St Julian's Church, off King Street. Above and around the stem are 24 finely carved figurines of saints, two of which are seen here.*

be seen on request at the local studies library in Norwich Central Library, across the road from the Theatre Royal.)

The best remaining part of the walls runs off steeply to the left from the end of Ber Street, followed by the line of Carrow Hill, a precipitous street which was laid down in the 1860s as a means of providing work for the unemployed.

A brief foray down Bracondale, Ber Street's continuation, provides a view of a pleasurable range of cherished Georgian terraces and individual houses, not least the Manor House (No. 54), 'caught as if in a time slip between Bracondale Court and a row of Regency houses', as Geoffrey Goreham describes it in his *Norwich Heritage*, a collection of newspaper articles published in book form in 1981. This warm, red-brick, Dutch-gabled building, dated 1578 on one of its gables, is a gentle feast of Tudor flamboyance, lovingly restored by two private owners after years of misuse.

The route down Carrow Hill passes the most substantial surviving walls and towers, the former 20 feet high and more than 3 feet thick. The upper tower is known as the **Black Tower** (**40**) because of its black flints. In the no-nonsense early 17th century, it was turned into a prison for 'unruly, infected persons'. At the bottom of Carrow Hill turn left into King Street. Immediately opposite is the old Colman factory (now part of a conglomerate), centred on the mansion occupied from the 1850s by J.J. Colman which was built amid the ruins of the nunnery of Carrow, one of the numerous Norwich religious houses suppressed by Henry VIII.

To the right is Carrow Bridge, the swing bridge over the Wensum. From there, on the downriver side, can be seen the stumps of the old boom towers, from which, when the city walls were intact, a boom or chain could be slung across to block the river. King Street, which runs from this point directly through to Tombland, is one of the most ancient ways in Norwich, and until the 18th century was known as Conesford (the name is perpetuated in one of the city's political wards), which derives from the Anglo-Saxon 'king's ford.'

Ignore the modern sweep of Rouen Road (this was driven through after the planners had been thwarted in their wish to widen King Street) and hug the wall of the old Ferry Boat public house, which bumbles eccentrically down to the river, on descending levels of ancient building and adapted boathouse.

Further along on the left is **St Etheldreda's Church**, today used as a wood sculptor's studio – appropriately, in a county and city of sumptuous medieval church roofs. The church dates back to Norman times (the nave south door hints at this) but has been much changed over the centuries. It was rescued from crumbling neglect by the Norwich Historic Churches Trust (who have 17 of the city's churches in their care). With a pretty, stumpy round tower and low-roofed nave and chancel it looks serene and attractive among its churchyard trees.

A short way down King Street, on the same side, is a handsome row of gabled, excellently restored medieval cottages, including the former Ship inn (note over the entrance to Ship Yard a fine 16th-century lintel inscribed for the Princes inn, in Princes Street, its original home). This is another testimony to the foresight of Norwich City Council, who in the early 1960s bought the houses when they were in poor condition and threatened by demolition, and brought them triumphantly back to life.

Immediately opposite is something altogether different and a yet more remarkable survival. Long known as the **Music House** (**39**), the face it presents to the street is Jacobean, with two huge, six-light windows side by side, topped by plain raised pediments, and above them smaller versions of the same style. This is the oldest dwelling house in Norwich, the 12th-century city residence and banking vault (attested by the splendid crypt, now a club and bar) of wealthy Jews whose function was to provide capital for the new Norman masters. Early documents describe it as the residence of Isaac the Jew. He must have been privileged to live here, for the Jewish ghetto was in the area between the Castle and the market place. The subsequent disappearance of the Jews from Norwich and elsewhere is part of the sad, long story of virulent anti-Semitism.

There was a particularly nasty anti-Jewish riot in Norwich in 1144, set off by the clearest piece of cynical invention, which produced a saint for the city – William of Norwich. Story has it that, in pursuance of some imagined beastly ritual, 12-year-old William, an apprentice boy, was abducted by Hebrews to be gagged, shaved, lacerated with a crown of thorns and crucified, in Holy Week of 1144. A nun discovered the body, says the tale, on Mousehold Heath, in a state of incorruption which afforded a sure sign of saintliness.

But it was not until the reign of Edward I, around the turn of the 14th century, that here and throughout England the real pogroms began, fostered by the Church, and the Jewish communities disappeared. Isaac's old house went through a series of hands, all distinguished. Sir John Paston (whose family we have already encountered in Elm Hill) reconstructed it in the late 15th century. In the 17th century, the great Chief Justice Coke, Recorder of Norwich, lived there (having married a Paston) and altered it, the great Jacobean windows presumably being part of his changes.

Its name today is Wensum Lodge, a popular further study and recreational centre. But to locals, it is still the Music House, a title established during the 16th to 18th centuries, when it was the meeting place of the Waits, the 'official' musicians of the city. Whether, as Norwich lore has it, they were originally given their instruments by Queen Elizabeth herself when she made her grand visit here in 1578 may be open to question. But it is certain that they were asked to accompany a major naval expedition against Cadiz, such was their reputation for excellence. The Waits were dissolved by the Corporation at the end of the 18th century. In this decade the tradition has been revived – crumhorns, shawms, sackbuts, livery and all.

In Chief Justice Coke's time and for many years after, King Street was one one of the grandest thoroughfares in the city; great town houses, with gardens extending down to the river, lined the roadway. Francis Blomefield, in his vast 18th-century undertaking, *The History of Norfolk*, says that here successively were the town houses of Sir Miles Stapleton (one of the original Knights of the Garter), Sir William Boleyn, Lady Anne Boleyn (pronounced 'Bullen') and the Cleres of Ormesby, and that part of the land belonged formerly to the Austin Friars.

Later King Street came into the hands of the Howards, Dukes of Norfolk – No. 97, on the corner of Mountergate, is still called Howard House. This was, in effect, the 'garden house' of the ducal residence. The topographer Thomas Baskerville described what he saw there when he visited Norwich in

42 *The watergate at Pull's Ferry once straddled the canal – filled in during the 18th century – which the Normans dug to transport imported Caen stone from the river to the Cathedral construction site. The present much-restored building dates from the 15th century; the ferry ran until the 1930s.*

1681: 'Taking a boat for pleasure to see the city by water, the boatman brought us to a fair garden belonging to the Duke of Norfolk, having handsome stairs leading to the water, by which we ascended into the garden and saw a good bowling green and many fine walks; the gardener now keeping good liquors and fruits to entertain such as come to see it.' By Blomefield's time the Howards had long since left Norwich, but he records that it was still called 'My Lord's Garden'.

Long before the Cokes and Howards, however, this was already the wealthy merchants' quarter. Further along the street on the Music House side is a long brick, tiled and half-timbered building which has been recognised for many years as an important medieval survivor. But only in 1987–8 was its true value rediscovered and revealed to the public under the appealing name of **Dragon Hall** (**37**).

Around 1450 Robert Toppes, Lord Mayor and a rich textile merchant, built at first-floor level a great hall, 80 feet by 21 feet, to display his goods and impress his customers. But after him came many changes. From private residence and merchant's town house and warehouse, the whole building was divided and subdivided into six cottages. It has served as inn, rectory and butcher's shop before again becoming an inn, the Old Barge.

Now the additions of centuries have been swept away to reveal the great hall once again, and in one of the spandrels of the magnificent roof, a carved and painted dragon. The objective is to use it as a Heritage Centre and perhaps as a centre-piece of a 'living museum', a re-creation of medieval, mercantile Norwich. Appropriately, Dragon Hall is approached through Old Barge Yard (and an imposing 14th-century doorway, said to have come from a nearby priory, though this is open to question), so the name by which it was known for so long will not be forgotten.

Immediately opposite Old Barge Yard is St Julian's Alley, leading to **St Julian's Church**, now celebrated for its association with Mother Julian of Norwich, the 14th-century anchoress who wrote one of the great masterpieces of spiritual literature, *Revelations of Divine Love* – the first known book in English written by a woman.

In 1942, during a particularly savage German air attack on Norwich, the church was virtually destroyed. But 11 years later it rose again, a beautiful and skilful blending of old and new. The stump of the round tower is Saxon, as are the two circular windows in the north wall of the nave. On the opposite side is a reconstruction of the cell where Mother Julian lived as a recluse. It is entered through a Norman doorway moved here from the ruins of St Michael at Thorn, a church a few hundred yards away which was entirely destroyed in the same air raid. The cell itself is simple, unadorned and wonderfully tranquil: a few minutes spent there is always a rewarding experience, a spiritual recharging of batteries.

The early-15th-century font (**41**) in this memorable little church came from the redundant All Saints' in Westlegate. Each panel of its octagonal bowl and base is filled with crisply carved figurines, 8 around the stem and 16 above. Among the assemblage of saints are Michael and George, the Apostles, Norfolk's own Walstan (the gentle farmer saint), and possibly also the 'martyred' William of Norwich. Note also the high-altar reredos, a 1930s piece from Oberammergau.

Sadly redundant, and with no alternative use yet found for it, is **St Peter Parmentergate**, further along on the same side as St Julian's. Its name, according to R.H. Mottram, dates back to the period when this immediate locality, taking advantage of small streams flowing from the higher ground on the Ber Street ridge, was occupied by parmenters – leather-dressers and parchment-makers. This once fine church is entirely Perpendicular, having been rebuilt in the late 15th century.

A particular treasure here is the Berney tomb, erected in 1623 to Richard and Elizabeth Berney, which the Norwich Historic Churches Trust zealously preserves as one of the finest monuments in the churches in its care. Under an imposing four-poster canopy, the couple lie stiffly, in prayer, richly dressed, with a splendid Berney and Hobart coat of arms between the canopy and the tomb slab.

Turn down Mountergate (a corruption of Parmentergate), across Rose Lane and Prince of Wales Road and into St Faith's Lane. At the junction of the lane with Recorder Road is a pleasant green, the site in times past of the horse fair. In the angle of the two roads is a delightful surprise, a small park which remains unknown even to many Norwich residents. The **James Stuart Garden** was opened in 1922 in memory of the man who came to Norwich, married a Colman, and devoted himself to advancing education for working people.

From the corner of the little 'horsefair' green, and beside Horsefair House, runs a pathway into the Lower Cathedral Close. In the Close turn right towards the river, and directly ahead is what must be the most photographed

43 Cow Tower, which stands strategically in a sharp angle of the River Wensum north-east of the Cathedral, was rebuilt in brick in 1399. This was a vulnerable point in the city's defences, since the walls did not extend along the river. Before the Dissolution of the monasteries the tower served as the prior's tollhouse to collect dues from vessels plying between city and coast.

building in all Norwich, **Pull's Ferry** (**42**), which dates from the 15th century. It marks the medieval watergate, access to a canal originally dug to bring the Caen stone for the Cathedral directly to the spot where it was needed; it continued to be used for ferrying supplies to the great monastic priory and was not finally filled in until late in the 18th century.

Now turn left along the pleasant riverside walk, part of an 8-mile pathway beside the Wensum, which the city council began in 1967 and continues to extend and link up. It runs from the boom towers at Carrow Bridge all the way to Hellesdon, in the city's north-west suburbs. Cross over Bishopgate, and at the sharp angle of the river you come to **Cow Tower** (**43**). For so long grazing beasts rubbed themselves against it and sheltered by it that it acquired its title by general usage, but the tower's original role was much more businesslike: it was the tollhouse, from which the servants of the Prior of Norwich collected toll from vessels plying the river between city and coast.

Back in Bishopgate, a turn to the left reveals **Bishop's Bridge** (**44**), oldest of the Norwich bridges and rich in historical associations. It was built in the 13th century by the Bishop and Prior – its existing arches are largely the original ones – and was controlled and maintained by them for more than a century until it passed into the hands of the city in 1393. Elizabeth I crossed over it to visit Mount Surrey, the Earl of Surrey's palace, built within the ruins of St Leonard's Priory, which occupied the high land at the top of what is now Gas Hill, behind the old gasometers. And less than 30 years earlier it had witnessed part of the worst violence and bloodshed which Norwich has

44 *Bishop's Bridge in its leafy setting at the end of Bishopgate, the oldest of the Norwich bridges. It was built in the 13th century by the Bishop and Prior, and in 1549 was the scene of fierce fighting during Kett's Rebellion.*

45 *The Adam and Eve in Bishopgate, with its Flemish gables, is a largely 16th-century building, but parts of the pub date back to 1247 and it claims to be the oldest hostelry in the city.*

ever known in its long history (for the city successfully avoided both the Wars of the Roses and the Parliamentary Wars).

On 7 July 1549 began in Wymondham, on a hot summer's day, what was to flare into Kett's Rebellion. The enclosure of common land was its basic cause, but it was fuelled by a whole series of agrarian and social grievances, which resulted in yeoman Robert Kett approaching Norwich with a raggle-taggle army of some twenty thousand, and his brother William, a butcher, as his lieutenant. They reached Bowthorpe on 10 July and the High Sheriff of Norfolk, Sir Edward Windham, rode out to parley with them – 'and only 'scaped by his horsemanship being better than his rhetorik'.

The rebels took up station on Mousehold Heath to the north-east of the city, major gentry were rounded up and Mount Surrey was overrun. Another week of negotiation followed. The King sent York Herald to call the rebels to order, but – story has it – one of his guards shot and killed a boy who made a rude gesture at the herald, and that was the signal for the real fighting to begin. The city was besieged; violent fighting took place on and around Bishop's Bridge, which 'the rebels stormed with desperate courage by swimming the river on either side of it in face of volleys of arrows', as one account records, and on they swept down Bishopgate to Palace Plain, where their story will be taken up again.

On the way they passed by the gates of the **Great Hospital (46)** and its **Church of St Helen**. This remarkable institution has survived, true to its conception as a sanctuary for the needy, the sick and the aged, since it was

founded in 1249 by Walter de Suffield, Bishop of Norwich, a Norfolk man celebrated for his charity. He provided for the support of a Master and 4 priests, 2 deacons, 4 sisters over 50 years old, all the 'poor and decrepit' chaplains in the diocese, and 13 poor people to be lodged there. In addition the Master of the Grammar School was to nominate 7 poor boys to have 'school dinners' daily.

Over the years its role has changed and adapted, but its vocation remains the same. To stroll through the Great Hospital grounds on a summer's day, around the cottages, old almshouses and gardens, is to experience the serenity of growing old in security.

The church at the centre of the Hospital is fascinating. A close look, as a 1949 official history put it, 'will reveal that chimneys rise from the ridge of the church and that liberties have been taken with some of its windows': the curious arrangement of former centuries, which prevailed until the 1960s, was that the chancel provided wards for women, and the nave for men, while the centre part and transept were set aside for worship. This at once explains the oddly truncated form of the interior.

The chancel, rebuilt about 1383, is very fine, particularly its roof, with beautiful carved bosses and 252 panels carrying paintings of the imperial two-headed eagle. Tradition has it that they were placed there (like the shield on the end of St Andrew's Church) in honour of Anne of Bohemia, who visited the Great Hospital in 1383. Nave, tower, Master's Lodgings and cloisters were rebuilt about 1450.

46 *Radiant with flowers in spring and summer, the tiny mid-15th-century cloister of the Great Hospital in Bishopgate is one of the hidden delights of Norwich.*

In the 1580s a series of meetings took place in the Master's Lodgings between the Master, Robert Harrison, and his old Cambridge friend, Robert Browne, who believed that Christians had the right to choose their own ministers and exercise their own discipline, without the interference of bishops. They established what was in effect the first English Congregational church, and began to attract up to a hundred people to their services. This was too much for the bishop over the road, and his wrath descended on the two men. Harrison fled to Holland and Browne was clapped into prison. The matter caused a great stir throughout the land and prompted Shakespeare, ever ready to slip a newsworthy reference into his plays, to put into the mouth of Sir Andrew Aguecheek in *Twelfth Night* the observation: 'I had as lief be a Brownist as a politician'.

Harrison and Browne must have been brave men, for they could not have been unaware that little more than 20 years earlier, twice in the summer of 1557, and twice again in the following year, heretics had been led along Bishopgate, past the Great Hospital Gates, to be burned to death in Lollard's Pit, a spot scooped out of the chalk hillside just beyond and above Bishop's Bridge.

No such shadows were in evidence when Elizabeth I arrived in Norwich in August 1578, stayed at the Bishop's Palace, rode past the Hospital to dine with the Earl of Surrey at Mount Surrey, and on her return reined in her horse at the hospital gate to receive an oration in Latin from Stephen Limbert, Master of the Grammar School. No doubt awed by his sovereign, the poor man was overcome. 'Be not afraid', said the lady graciously. Whereupon Master Limbert launched into his speech. It is recorded that the Queen (herself no mean scholar of Latin) was delighted, and exclaimed: 'It is the best that I ever heard; you shall have my hand', and pulling off her glove, gave him her hand to kiss.

Gloriana's route back to the city, and the gates of the Bishop's Palace, would have taken her past the **Adam and Eve** pub (**45**) on the right. Rebuilt in her time, it dates back to 1247. Today, with its Flemish gables, flint walls and small-scale, cosy interior, it is a place of real character, and proudly upholds its claim to be the oldest hostelry in the city.

Bishopgate here swings sharply to the left, passing the new law courts on the right. Directly ahead is the redundant church of **St Martin at Palace**, a 14th- and 15th-century building, incorporating both Decorated and Perpendicular styles, which has suffered much from Victorian restoration. An interesting architectural curiosity is the range of diminutive, trefoil-shaped, clerestory windows to each side of the nave. Recently extensive archaeological work inside the church has revealed the outline of the former outer walls of an earlier church dating back to the 11th century.

Now work is in hand to transform St Martin's into a Probation Day Centre, a plan welcomed by the Norwich Historic Churches Trust 'because the social purpose is so positive and valuable', and equally because the architect's proposed plan 'is so sympathetic to the interior...and will enable the visitor to admire its beauties'. Among those beauties is the fine tomb chest of Lady Elizabeth Calthorpe, who died in 1578 – a great stone table, decorated with coloured shields, in an arched recess.

Immediately opposite St Martin's is the fortress-like gateway – leading to Bishop's House and the former Bishop's Palace – erected by Bishop Alnwick in the early 1430s (he was translated to Lincoln in 1436). At that time there lived, across the plain in his town house, that grand old man Sir Thomas Erpingham (immortalised by Shakespeare in *Henry V*), who commanded the bowmen at Agincourt. All that remains now of his early-14th-century mansion is the tall, six-light window which has been incorporated into the remodelled, restored building facing the tower of St Martin's.

The principal building on Palace Plain is **Cotman House**, a dignified, severe Georgian mansion of three superbly balanced storeys. Here in 1824 John Sell Cotman, the brilliant water-colourist of the Norwich School of painters, opened his 'School for Drawing and Painting in Water-colours. Terms one guinea and a half the quarter'. Clearly his income was not enough to maintain the establishment, for after ten worrying years he was evicted because of debts. Beside the house is an attractive 16th-century dormered pub, formerly the White Lion, now the Wig and Pen in acknowledgement of the new law courts. Both buildings were threatened with demolition in the 1930s. Happily they have survived planners and German bombs and are now fully restored.

This square was the scene of the fiercest fighting of Kett's Rebellion, in July and August 1549. Having crossed the river and reached Palace Plain, the rebels were brought to a halt at the edge of Tombland, where the Deputy Mayor, Augustine Steward, had set up defence lines. From London came the Marquis of Northampton with armoured knights, Italian mercenaries and others, said to number about fourteen hundred. In bitter action, the rebels fought magnificently but were pushed back (though they did capture the head of the Italian brigade – and hanged him in full view of the city).

Soon they attacked again, and once more Palace Plain was 'the front'; losses were bad on both sides. The death of Lord Sheffield marked the turning point. Just beyond St Martin's – a modern plaque in the wall of the Close marks the spot – he was dragged from his horse and brutally clubbed to death. In London the Privy Council acted with speed, and despatched the Earl of Warwick with an army which had been preparing for an expedition into Scotland. He arrived in Norwich about 23 August and used concentrated gunfire (his force included a detachment of Swiss *arquebusiers* armed with heavy, portable matchlock guns) to clear the city. The rebels withdrew to their camp on Mousehold Heath but, inexplicably, threw away this advantage, advanced to meet the royal army, and at 'Dussens Dale', on the lower part of Mousehold, were cut to pieces. The Kett brothers fled but were captured, Robert to be hung from the battlements of Norwich Castle, William to be strung from the church steeple in his home town of Wymondham.

Much of the bloodshed took place before the doors of the Maid's Head Hotel, which was already old then. It is said to stand on the site of the original Bishop's Palace, and traces of masonry from that period have been found. This was the departure point, in 1762, of the first regular stage coach to London, 'The Norwich Machine'. On a plinth in front of the Maid's Head is a memorial bust to Edith Cavell, the heroic Norfolk-born nurse who, while serving as a hospital matron in Belgium during the First World War, was arrested by the Germans for helping Allied prisoners to escape. She was shot by firing squad in 1915. Her body lies in Life's Green beyond the presbytery of the Cathedral.

Over the road, the eye is caught by the massive, ungainly male versions

47 *Augustine Steward's House, leaning precariously over Tombland Alley, is a half-timbered mansion of great character which was built by the Norwich worthy who held Kett's rebels at bay in 1549. The raised areas in the foreground, now covered in grass, are said to contain the heaped-up bones of plague victims.*

of caryatids which support the porchway of what generations of Norwich people have known as the Samson and Hercules Hall, or more familiarly, the Sam 'n' 'erc. At its heart is a medieval manor house, built by Sir John Fastolf. But it has undergone many severe alterations through the years, and is now a dance hall.

Much more picturesque is the half-timbered, lopsided house facing the lower Cathedral gate. This is **Augustine Steward's House** (**47**), built in 1549 by the same worthy merchant who held Kett's rebels at bay. Later he moved to Elm Hill, where he built again. The quaint angularities of this building seem to have occurred in very recent times – paintings and drawings before the middle of the last century show it reasonably upright.

Through the archway under the house is Tombland Alley, a hive of local lore where fable and fact are indistinguishable. The raised areas to each side of the pathway (**47**) are said to contain the remains of layers upon layers of plague victims (of the Black Death, in 1349, when the city and county were cruelly depopulated? or the outbreak which Queen Elizabeth left behind in 1578, which claimed a quarter of the city's population?). At the bend in the alley round the tower of St George Tombland Church, the base of the tower 'steps' out like a broad shelf: the more enthusiastic of Kett's rebels, by all accounts, trussed up their prisoners and dropped them head first onto it from the top of the tower. Small wonder that a little grey lady is said to float unhappily up Tombland Alley and disappear through a wall.

St George's Church, in its lovely corner setting, is one of the most attractive churches in the city, dating from the mid-15th century. The tower, which can be dated precisely, through legacies, to 1445, is particularly good – tall and slim and beautifully decorated with chequerwork. The two-storey south porch has a centre boss showing the church's patronal saint, and there are more representations of him inside.

The pleasing interior has numerous excellent details (**48**), including bird-like angels at the foot of the chancel wall-posts, a notable early-18th-century reredos, and a very good pulpit of the same period, complete with delicate staircase and tester and, on the front, an arresting 'sun in splendour' in ivory around the IHS sacred monogram. The monument to Alderman Anguish (d. 1617), hidden away by the organ, is worth a look – he was a great beneficiary to the city and is remembered in the Anguish Charity, which is still a generous patron of educational causes. St George's is also the setting for a regular series of concerts, and gives a platform to young musicians on the threshold of their careers.

Running along the churchyard is Princes Street, which merits a short diversion for a view, towards the top of Elm Hill, of one of the city's most

48 *St George's Church, Tombland: the memorial to John Symonds (d. 1609), 'who has given by his last tastament unto ye pore of this parish two shillings a week to continue for ever'.*

49 *The beautiful Erpingham Gate into the Upper Close of the Cathedral, built about 1420, recalls a gallant son of Norwich, old Sir Thomas Erpingham, the commander of the archers at Agincourt (1415). His statue in the central niche stands over the finely carved mouldings and polygonal buttresses.*

picturesque prospects. The 16th-century house a few yards up on the right, with herring-bone brickwork and exposed timbers, was claimed by a pre-war local historian to be part of the White Horse inn, where in the early 17th century many touring companies of players appeared (with the less than gracious consent of the mayor).

The rowdyism of theatrical 'rogues and vagabonds' was as nothing to the scenes experienced in Tombland a few centuries earlier, when in 1272 the long-smouldering animosity between the Cathedral priory and the town broke out into open warfare. Scant records indicate that the Prior's soldiers and monks set up some sort of armament upon a bell tower, the better to bombard the town and its people. The enraged citizenry broke in from Tombland, and in the ensuing mayhem monks and retainers were killed on one side, townsfolk on the other, huge damage was done and extensive parts of the priory buildings, and of the Cathedral itself, were put to the fire.

The disturbance was serious enough for the King himself to hie to East Anglia and mete out justice. The arsonists who could be identified were savagely punished, as was the city itself: privileges which had been granted in earlier charters were withdrawn, a swingeing fine of 3000 marks was imposed, and the Mayor was given a spell in the Tower. The King called the Prior to account too, indicating clearly that it was six of one and half a dozen of the other.

Retribution was not complete, however. Soon after 1300. Norwich was made to build the upper gateway into the Close, the **Ethelbert Gate** (**1**, **52**), as a further penance. Above the gateway is a room which became the chapel of

51 *Admiral Nelson's statue (by Thomas Milnes, 1847) in the Upper Close looks towards the school where, for a brief period, he was a pupil.*

50 *The early-14th-century Carnary Chapel of the King Edward VI School in the Upper Cathedral Close, distinguished by a spacious undercroft, with large, circular windows. The 14th- and 15th-century origins of the school buildings to the left have been obscured by the 1830s façade, but the medieval doorway remains, as does the 16th-century Flemish gable to the right.*

St Ethelbert, to replace the church of that name within the Close which the mob destroyed in their riot. In the early 1980s the room was restored and made comfortable to provide a charming meeting room. It is also used for rehearsals by Norfolk's internationally known choir, the Broadland Singers, and has been appropriately re-named The Barbirolli Room.

At the lower end of Tombland is the beautiful **Erpingham Gate** (**49**), built about 1420, and a continuing reminder of Sir Thomas Erpingham, who lived round the corner in Palace Plain. The rich decoration of the gate – 24 saints in the deep mouldings of the arch, opulently carved buttresses and spandrels, and over all, a figure of Sir Thomas kneeling in a crocketted niche – has come through the centuries unscathed. Even the appalling vandalism and sacrilege in the Cathedral itself during the Puritan period passed it by. One would like to believe R.H. Mottram's assertion that the gate and its figures were protected by 'Sir Thomas's good name'.

Through the Erpingham Gate there is a splendid view of the west end of the **Cathedral**, its immense soaring Perpendicular window and great west door belying the essentially Norman building. Both window and door were inserted during the 1420s–1430s by Bishop Alnwick (the same prelate who built the fortress-gate to the palace), whose arms are in the door's spandrels. To the left is **King Edward VI School** (**50**). The curious porch with ascending steps, leading to a chapel, was added by Bishop Lyhart in the mid-15th century. The lower part of the chapel was originally the charnel house, where surplus bones from churchyards in the Close and city were placed. The

52 A handsome Georgian 'gentleman's residence' (now converted to offices) in a corner of the Upper Close, adjacent to the Ethelbert Gate.

53 Near the west end of the Cathedral stands this remnant of the monastic buildings which disappeared at the Reformation.

54, 55 *The beauty of the old houses in the Lower Cathedral Close is matched by their trees and gardens. Left: Looking down Hook's Walk, a lane of picturesque angles, gables and textures. Right: No. 34 Lower Close, at one time the bakehouse and later an inn.*

OVERLEAF
56 *Looking eastward down the nave of Norwich Cathedral – a breathtaking view of the powerful Norman arcades and magnificent 15th-century roof.*
57 *The superlative lierne-vaulted roof of the nave, built by Bishop William Lyhart in the mid-15th century after a disastrous fire, is enriched by a wonderful collection of roof bosses.*

school was established as the King Edward VI Grammar School in 1553, but it claims descent from an earlier medieval foundation. It has produced many famous men – among them Admiral Lord Nelson, though his stay as a pupil was a very short one. His statue (**51**), set on a high plinth and framed by trees opposite the chapel, looks impassively towards the school.

Pass between Nelson and the Cathedral, noting the Cathedral Visitors' Centre (a laudably skilful and sensitive conversion into a welcoming coffee shop) and vestiges of the priory ruins (**53**), and follow a route along the **Upper Close** and then left towards the **Lower Close**. Here the wide green is surrounded by some of the most beautiful houses in all Norwich (**52**).

A leap of imagination is needed to accept that this square formed the centre of the priory's practical affairs. Immediately facing you, at the lower end, is a lovely, mellow grouping reconstructed in 1682 from the monastery brewhouses. The left-hand end of the range (**55**) long served as a public house, the Three Cranes – not the elegant birds, but the derricks which hoisted stone and grain from the barges which reached this point on the canal-cut from Pull's Ferry.

The dignifed terrace on the left was once granaries, a bakery and stores, with shelter for the swineherd and accommodation appropriate to his rank for the steward. Between the two groups of houses, in the far left corner, runs **Hook's Walk** (**54**), with more picturesque angles, gables and textures. The house on the left, built in 1661, standing out on little classical pillars, was from 1792 to 1817 the home of Dr Sayer, a locally celebrated scholar.

We retrace our steps, past the 'granary range', and turn right. On the left,

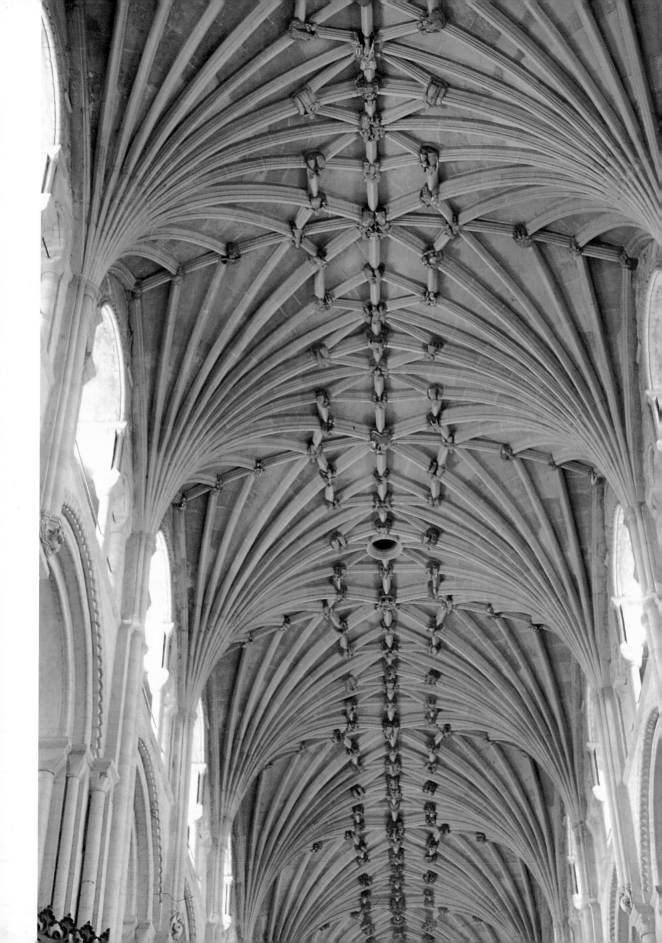

a car-park occupies the site of the monastic infirmary, whose remains can be seen. Continue on past the Deanery on the right (the original Prior's House) towards the south transept. From here there is a marvellous view of the late-15th-century spire and of the presbytery's great Decorated clerestory windows and elegant flying buttresses. The windows were built in the mid-14th century after the original spire had collapsed. A century later, the buttresses were added to support Bishop Goldwell's noble stone roof.

Go into the Cathedral through the south transept door. Pass through the transept and turn left into the nave south aisle, heading for the west end of the nave, from which point the view of the full length of the building is breathtaking, and the essentially Norman structure is powerfully apparent (**56**, **58**). The superlative roof of the nave (**56**, **57**), lierne vaulted, was built by William Lyhart (bishop 1446–72) after a disastrous fire in 1463. Walk down to the great screen on which the organ sits. The right-hand spandrel of the centre doorway contains the bishop's rebus (a personal badge punning on the owner's name), a hart lying down by rippling water. In the other spandrel is a bull, an emblem from his coat of arms. Look up high on each side, and on the corbels between the triforium arches you will see the same emblems, repeated alternately, this time carved in relief in stone.

Now go up the north aisle to the north transept, which also has fine roof vaulting. Another fire ravaged the Cathedral in 1509, and Bishop Nix re-roofed both transepts in stone. More than four centuries later this was to be the salvation of the building, for when German incendiary bombs fell onto the Cathedral in June 1942, their fire failed to catch. From the transept, walk round the apsidal east end and its side chapels. Here behind the high altar is the bishop's Saxon throne, a survival unique in Europe.

St Luke's Chapel (1100), in the south ambulatory, is a curious and attractive anomaly, a parish church in its own right. From the time of the building of the Cathedral by Bishop Herbert de Losinga – work began in 1096 – the people living and working in the Close had their own church, St Mary in the Marsh. At the Dissolution it was pulled down (the first dean sold the materials) and as compensation the parishioners were allowed to use the Cathedral's south aisle. Thirty years later they were moved on to St Luke's Chapel, and there they have remained ever since. Their font, which they brought with them from St Mary's, is one of the unusual seven-sacrament fonts peculiar to this part of England. Nearly all dating from the 15th century, they have eight carved panels, seven depicting the seven holy ordinances or sacraments (baptism, mass, confirmation, confession/penance, ordination to holy orders, marriage, and extreme unction) and the eighth the baptism or crucifixion of Christ. The St Mary in the Marsh example is much defaced, but remains a rich piece.

Here also is the Despencer reredos, which was probably given as a thank-offering for the victory of the 'fighting bishop', Henry Despencer, in the Peasants' Revolt of 1381. For many years this marvellous work of medieval painting – now superbly restored to its jewel-like colours – was used upside down as a table-top, before it was rediscovered in 1847.

Henry Despencer was a remarkable figure. He was in London when the Peasant's Revolt broke out in Norfolk. He hurried back, donned armour, mounted his horse, and is said personally to have led the charge against the insurgents' position near North Walsham. He seized Listester, the ringleader;

58 *The unforgettable Norman architecture of Norwich Cathedral – a view of the triforium of the presbytery.*

OVERLEAF

59 *The vast, nine-light west window of Norwich Cathedral was inserted in the early 15th century by Bishop Alnwick, who also built the fortress gate to the Bishop's Palace. The glass is mid-19th century, by the leading stained-glass artist of the time, George Hedgeland, and is one of the finest examples of his work.*

60 *The latten lectern of the pelican in her piety is Flemish work of about 1450; the Bishop's chair was designed by J.L. Pearson and made by a local North Walsham firm in 1895. In the background is the south side of the presbytery and Bishop Goldwell's magnificent tomb.*

61 *A shaft of sunlight catches the opulent and intricate wood carving over one of the canons' stalls in the choir. The stalls date largely from about 1420, in the time of Bishop Wakeryng, whose figure can be seen over the north-west door of the cloister.*

in his role of priest, shrived him (heard his confession and gave him absolution); and as judge condemned him and had him hanged, drawn and quartered.

Within the encircling ambulatory is the presbytery (**58**, **60**) and more soaring Norman artistry; the Caen stone here has a beautiful pink flush, infused by one of the great fires which struck the Cathedral in medieval times. Above is Bishop Goldwell's splendid 15th-century roof, studded with bosses which bear his rebus – a gilded well. Under one of the arches between presbytery and south ambulatory is his gorgeous tomb (**60**), crowned with an enormous golden well. (What appears to be foliage tumbling out of it is in fact fountaining water.)

Between nave and presbytery is the choir, a treasure-house of craftsmanship in wood. Intricate and exquisite detail is lavished on the canopies over the canons' stalls (**61**), and the scenes carved on the ancient misericords (the ledges underneath the hinged seats of the stalls) are an exuberant riot of medieval life and inspiration. They include a grumpy and mitred bishop; a monk thrashing a small boy over his knee; Samson enthusiastically hauling apart a lion's jaws; and a housewife chasing a fox that has stolen her goose, while a pig feeds from her pot in the mêlée.

OVERLEAF

63 *One of the wonderful collection of nearly four hundred roof bosses in the cloisters: Christ Crucified, in the east walk.*

64 *A detail of the superbly carved prior's door (c.1310) between the north-east corner of the cloisters and the Cathedral. Christ in glory is flanked by angels, supported in turn by a king and a bishop and Moses and St John.*

86

For many thousands of people who visit Norwich Cathedral, one of the particular glories of the building is at best only partly recognised, and it is immediately above our heads. In choir, presbytery, transepts, nave and cloisters, there are no fewer than 1005 carved and painted **roof bosses (63, 66)**, some 700 of them telling stories and parts of stories within their limited but remarkably complex spans. They raise a fascinating and thus far unanswered question: Why did story bosses begin here in Norwich, and at this particular time, and nowhere else in Christendom? Even when the practice spread, Norwich was to remain supreme in the number and variety of its bosses.

The earliest are in the **cloisters,** the magnificent 180-foot square walk approached from the south aisle, which was begun about 1297–1300 upon the ruins of the fired and pillaged priory left behind after the violent battle between town and monastery in 1270 and eventually completed in about 1430.

62 *The north-west corner of the cloisters of Norwich Cathedral, completed about 1430, clearly shows the abrupt change in the style of the window traceries, from Decorated (the two windows on the left) to Perpendicular, brought about by the interruption of building during the Black Death.*

This long progression is especially visible in the traceries of the open window arcades. The attractive Decorated designs of the first half of the 14th century reach a peak of flowing beauty – then stop, as can best be seen by standing in the south walk and looking across to the north-west corner of the north walk (**62**). This halt marks the coming in 1349 of the Black Death, the great plague which devastated the population of Norwich and Norfolk, as it did most of Britain and western Europe. Here in the cloisters, there was a lull of 60 years before work began again, such had been the effect of the

65 *These richly canopied 14th-century recesses next to the prior's door in the north-east corner of the cloisters served the monks as book cupboards.*

plague. And when it did, the new Perpendicular style took over, though with a little mixing of the old and new before the new emerged in its pure form.

But the east walk came first. The eloquently traceried double door at the centre of the walk led into the chapter house, which disappeared in the Dissolution. The roof bosses in the cloister vaulting at this point are all foliate – hawthorn, vine, oak and strawberry, with little images creeping into the foliage. The filled-in doorway to the left of the chapter house door, with its flowing lines and gilding, led into the muniments room or 'slype', where the manuscripts were kept.

Move northwards; the centre boss of the bay immediately after the slype door illustrates the Flagellation (whipping) of Christ, set against vine leaves and grapes. To its right, against the wall, St John is seen with his eagle emblem and a scroll. In the next bay, the centre boss shows Christ carrying his cross and inclining it towards Mary; immediately preceding, on the centre rib, is a wonderful green man (an old pagan image, probably representing the spirit of fertility, and much used in medieval Christian iconography), all eyes and tendrils. To the right of Christ with his cross is St Luke with his ox symbol; to the left, in stark contrast, a man and his wife (?) are involved in the bloodiest of domestic battles, he with a knife and she with a bludgeon.

In the next bay at the centre is Christ Crucified (**63**), with oak leaves coming out of the foot and the branches of the cross; to the right, St Matthew and an angel; to the left, cheery figures with pipe and tabor. Move on a bay further: here is a Resurrection with angels, bounded to the right by Mark and his lion emblem, and to the left by two men battling on horseback. Follow on along the centre rib to see two lions fighting each other; a naked figure is tied up, presumably for delivery to hell; and Christ with stigmata on hands and feet pulls the redeemed from the gaping jaws of a marvellous leviathan.

In the north-east corner of the cloisters, the focal point is the superb prior's doorway (**64**). Its richly carved frieze of figures and tabernacle canopies shows Christ in glory at the centre, flanked by angels, who are supported in turn by a king and a bishop and Moses and St John. To the right, the opulently canopied 14th-century recesses were book cupboards (**65**). Notice on the lower of the two benches below them, and further along too, at the right-hand end of the bench in the Christ Crucified bay, the scratched-in counters game, Nine Men's Morris, set out in a frame pattern marked by little 'button' indentations. The game is mentioned in *A Midsummer Night's Dream* but it was already old when Shakespeare was alive. It is nice to know that the scholarly monks were human, and enjoyed frivolous diversions.

Round the corner in the north walk, the bosses represent the last phase of work on the cloisters, dating from about 1430. Of particular interest, eight bays westward counting from the prior's door, is a complex five-scenes-in-one boss representing Salome's veil dance, Herod and his queen at table, John the Baptist before his execution, the execution itself, and Salome bearing John's head on a platter. In the next bay comes a trio of bosses depicting the story of Thomas à Becket; and two bays on again (third from the west end) against the wall, a gorgeous two-in-one interpretation of the martyrdom of St Denis, patron saint of Paris: he is seen robed and mitred, awaiting the headman's blow; then decapitated, serenely carrying his own severed head, on which the mitre sits undisturbed.

The coats of arms painted on the north wall, replaced during this century, are (as far as is known) those of the great landed families of Norfolk who dined in the cloisters with Elizabeth I when she visited in 1578, and who left their armorial bearings here as a memento.

In the south-west corner of the cloisters, under carved canopies, is a curiosity, the open troughs where throughout the year the monks washed before meals. The idea of working, walking and washing in these open walks, throughout a Norfolk winter, is a sobering thought. The royal figures set in the ancient niches over the troughs look mildly out of time and place. They represent George VI and Queen Elizabeth (now the Queen Mother), marking the fact that the Queen came here in 1938 to re-open the cloisters after restoration.

Immediately in front of the washbasins is a roof boss which is worth attention, though to appreciate its detail one must move round anti-clockwise with well-craned neck. It shows a Norfolk windmill complete with miller; a woman on horseback with a sack of corn slung over her shoulders; birds feeding on the corn stubble; a grove of trees; and a little house, tucked up into the groin of the roof. Over the immediately adjacent doorway, note the fine Adam and Eve and the serpent wound round a tree.

As you return to the Cathedral via the north-west cloister door, notice at the head of its archway Bishop John Wakeryng, dying reverently and being ministered to by angels. He was partly responsible for the fine choir stalls, though history remembers him more as Lord Keeper of the Great Seal, and a man of strict views who forbade barbers to shave their customers on Sundays – except during harvest.

On the sanctuary and presbytery roofs the bosses are an orderly storm of golden wells, echoing Bishop Goldwell's rebus crowning his sumptuous tomb below. There are more fine examples in the transepts. But it is over the choir and organ screen, and continuing right to the west end, that the truly staggering collection comes. First, at the extreme east end, abutting the tower crossing, a magnificent golden sun with an imperious face – according to modern scholarship, it is the Sun of York, a tactful bow in the direction of the new regime. For this work was begun in the late 1460s under the inspiration of Bishop Lyhart after the fire of 1463; Edward IV was on the throne, having crushed the Lancastrians and seized the Crown in 1466.

Here in this first bay, the sun's light, and that of God, red robed with a unicorn beside him and compasses in his hand, shines on animal creation: an eagle, a fish, a white hart, and a swan with a coronet round its neck (which could refer to the insignia of Richard II). Adam and Eve are here too, with a very female serpent, the coils winding down from a human torso. The Tree stands in a pot. Why? – so that it might be carried about, as in the mystery play which each year was performed here as part of the Norwich Cycle.

The second depicts Noah and a wonderful ark with animals peering through the portholes, a unicorn among them. On the tangents round this centre-piece, the ark is being built; Cain whirls the jaw bone of an ass with which he will kill Abel; a girl with tucked-up skirt carries into the ark a tray of cocks and hens; one of Noah's sons carries a ram on his back and a ewe under his arm; Noah, merry with wine and egged on by his sons, exposes himself, fulsomely; the body of a drowned spotted horse is fed on by a raven; and when the flood abates, Noah plants a vineyard, vivid in red, gold and green.

The next bay tells the stories of Abraham, Isaac and Jacob. The highlight here is the Tower of Babel, shown as a very medieval castle. Nearby, Jacob's mother puts a hairy beard upon him so that he can steal his brother Esau's birthright, and behind them stands an elegant Norwich house of the mason/artist's day.

Jacob and his life fill the fourth bay; Joseph is the focus of the next, particularly good being the boss on which his brothers shove him enthusiastically into a well which looks like a circular bath. The sixth bay features Moses and Pharaoh, including a remarkably lively Red Sea scene in which Pharaoh is armoured like Richard III at Bosworth Field, and sinks below the waves beside a chariot whose 15th-century Yarmouth cart outline is not masked by its gilding.

Bay seven is largely David's tale, but includes a vigorous Samson carrying off the golden gates of Gaza, one under each arm. David and Solomon, ancestors of Christ, provide the link between Old and New Testaments, and in bay eight the Annunciation, the Nativity and Herod provide the themes, including an all too graphic Massacre of the Innocents.

There are yet six bays to go, taking in the Flight into Egypt, Christ's Passion (**66**), Resurrection and Ascension, and a final bay of warnings and examples for weak and mortal man.

Places of Interest on the City Outskirts

Mousehold Heath

Overlooking Norwich on the north-east side is Mousehold Heath, a splendid 190-acre expanse of heath and woodland, from whose highest points there are fine vantages over the city – something not lost on Robert Kett and his rebels, when in 1549 they made their camp there before swooping down to besiege the town. One of the best views is from Britannia Road, opposite Britannia Barracks. Formerly the land belonged to the Church, but in 1880 it was handed over to the city on condition that it be used, for ever, for the recreation of the people.

The University of East Anglia

The University of East Anglia occupies the site of a former golf course at Earlham on the western edge of the city. The construction of its great spread of concrete buildings, linked by open, elevated walkways, began in the mid-1960s and took several years to complete. Designed by Denys Lasdun, with additions by Bernard Fielden, the angular blocks and ziggurats have attracted extremes of response. More than 20 years on, the expanses of concrete have stained rather than mellowed – though the superbly maintained grounds, with tree plantations and a man-made broad (lake) adjoining the River Yare, have done much to soften the outlines. On the river edge of the campus, work began in 1976 on the **Sainsbury Centre** (**67**), a shimmering glass and aluminium structure by Foster Associates. It is variously regarded as a masterpiece of modern architectural sculpture or as a glorified aircraft hanger. It houses the distinguished personal collection of Robert and Lisa Sainsbury, which ranges from primitive ethnic art to work by contemporary masters. Between the campus and the Norwich–Watton road is Earlham Hall, now the University's School of Law, a most attractive building dating from 1642. For more than a century (up to 1896) it was a Gurney residence and the childhood home of Elizabeth Fry, Quaker and zealous prison reformer.

Index of Streets, Buildings and Places

Numbers in heavy type refer to illustrations.

CENT

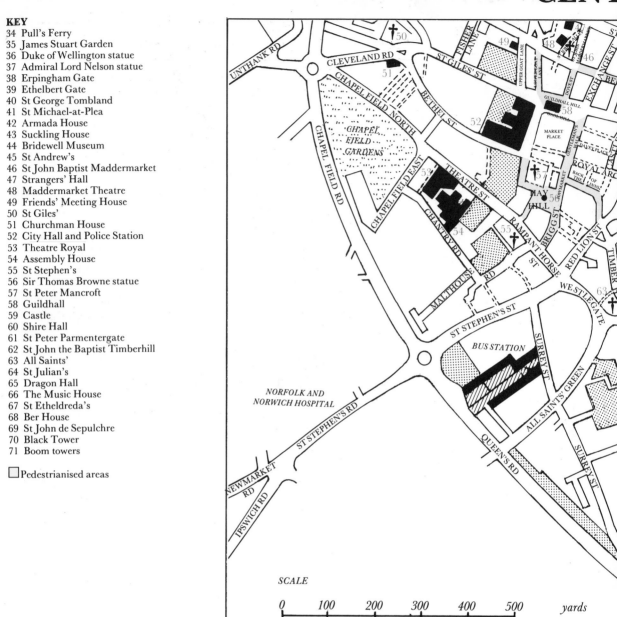

KEY

34 Pull's Ferry
35 James Stuart Garden
36 Duke of Wellington statue
37 Admiral Lord Nelson statue
38 Erpingham Gate
39 Ethelbert Gate
40 St George Tombland
41 St Michael-at-Plea
42 Armada House
43 Suckling House
44 Bridewell Museum
45 St Andrew's
46 St John Baptist Maddermarket
47 Strangers' Hall
48 Maddermarket Theatre
49 Friends' Meeting House
50 St Giles'
51 Churchman House
52 City Hall and Police Station
53 Theatre Royal
54 Assembly House
55 St Stephen's
56 Sir Thomas Browne statue
57 St Peter Mancroft
58 Guildhall
59 Castle
60 Shire Hall
61 St Peter Parmentergate
62 St John the Baptist Timberhill
63 All Saints'
64 St Julian's
65 Dragon Hall
66 The Music House
67 St Etheldreda's
68 Ber House
69 St John de Sepulchre
70 Black Tower
71 Boom towers

☐ Pedestrianised areas